TARGET AFRICA

Obianuju Ekeocha

TARGET AFRICA

Ideological Neocolonialism of the Twenty-First Century

With a Foreword by Robert P. George

IGNATIUS PRESS   SAN FRANCISCO

Cover art and design by Enrique J. Aguilar Pinto

© 2018 by Ignatius Press, San Francisco
All rights reserved
ISBN 978-1-62164-215-2 (PB)
ISBN 978-1-64229-530-6 (eBook)
Library of Congress Control Number 2017955106
Printed in the United States of America ∞

To my beloved parents,
Christopher and Comfort,
whose love and support have sustained me
through the hills and valleys of life

CONTENTS

Foreword, by Robert P. George   9

Introduction   13

1   Population Control   31

2   The Hypersexualization of Youth   59

3   The Seeds of Radical Feminism   77

4   The Push for Abortion Rights   97

5   The Normalization of Homosexuality   119

6   Modern-Day Colonial Masters   137

7   Aid Addiction   157

8   Toward the Decolonization of Africa   175

Conclusion   195

Appendix: An African Woman's Open Letter
to Melinda Gates   197

Index   205

FOREWORD

It is sometimes said that the people of sub-Saharan Africa and other developing parts of the world live in "post-colonial" societies.

I wish it were true.

The fact is that colonialism for the people and peoples of Africa and other places did not really end, or, if it ended, it has been reinstituted. Today's colonialism lacks the formal features of the old colonialism—there are no longer viceroys, governors general, and occupying armies—but it is nevertheless a type of colonialism—ideological colonialism. The economically powerful and culturally dominant nations whose governing ideology is a form of what the late Robert Bellah described as "expressive individualism", use their hegemonic power to impose on the people of Africa and other developing nations and regions legal and cultural norms informed by that ideology—despite the fact that expressive individualism and its legal and cultural norms are not just "foreign" but are antithetical to the beliefs and values of those on whom the hegemons seek to impose them.

In the book you now hold, the great Nigerian human rights activist Obianuju Ekeocha casts a spotlight on the new colonialism and subjects it to searching critical scrutiny. She shows, for example, how in the name of "human rights" the basic right to life of the unborn child is being daily undermined by Western governments and by (often partially government-funded) "nongovernmental organizations", such as International Planned Parenthood, who push abortion. Similarly, the pro-fertility and pro-marriage and family beliefs of vast numbers of Africans and others are undermined in the name of "human rights", as that term is (mis)used by advocates of population control, sexual permissiveness, certain forms of self-styled feminism, and the redefinition of marriage to eliminate the norm of sexual complementarity.

Expressive individualism is at the heart of the secular progressive worldview that now functions as the religion of many Western elites. It is increasingly clear that it is a militant, evangelizing, and fundamentalist type of "religion". It seeks to embody its core doctrines in law as well as social practices, and it exhibits very little tolerance, or even patience, for dissent or dissenters. It regards "traditional" beliefs and values—from the sanctity of human life in all stages and conditions, to the ideal of chastity and the idea of marriage as the conjugal union of husband and wife, to the conviction that children are blessings that are far more valuable than personal economic advancement or material possessions and wealth—as retrograde and benighted. Such beliefs and values are to be stamped out among allegedly "backward" people and peoples as quickly and efficiently as practicable. Where possible, Western elites are willing to accomplish the goal by conditioning various forms of aid on conformity to expressive individualist ideology. If necessary, they are prepared to use international legal institutions to attempt to coerce the "backward" into compliance.

Can the people and peoples of Africa and other developing parts of the world stand up to those to whom Obianuju Ekeocha calls "our new colonial masters"? Is resistance possible—or is it futile? The task is anything but easy. The "power imbalance" between the two sides—especially

given the financial resources available to the neocolonial-
ists for their projects—is daunting, to say the least. But
the human values and moral principles for which people
like Obianuju Ekeocha stand possess the luminosity and
power of truth. That does not guarantee their success, but
it gives the resistance forces genuine power, albeit not of
a material kind.

What these forces also need is the support of good people in the West who have themselves refused to yield to
the hegemonic power of secular progressivism and expressive individualism. Ekeocha's fellow Africans and others
need to know that many Christians and other men and
women of goodwill in the developed world stand with
them, not with their "new colonial masters". We need
to be the counterweight to those who purport to speak
in our name and who use our tax money to undermine
the human values and moral principles that we share with
countless people in the developing world—people who do
not want to go down the secular progressive path that
so many developed societies have gone down.

Robert P. George
McCormick Professor of Jurisprudence
Princeton University
Princeton, New Jersey

INTRODUCTION

A Child of an Independent Country

I was born twenty years after my country, Nigeria, became independent. My five older siblings and I were raised in a postcolonial climate of hope, national pride, and patriotism. We were taught, at home and at school, to appreciate our national heritage and our cultural traditions.

At the tender age of four, I learned the national anthem, which my schoolmates and I sang every morning on the assembly ground of Alvan Nursery School:

> Arise, O compatriots,
> Nigeria's call obey
> To serve our fatherland
> With love and strength and faith.
> The labor of our heroes past
> Shall never be in vain.
> To serve with heart and might
> One nation bound in freedom,
> Peace, and unity.
>
> O God of creation,
> Direct our noble cause
> And guide our leaders right.
> Help our youth the truth to know
> In love and honesty to grow,
> And living just and true

Great lofty heights attain
To build a nation where peace
And justice shall reign.

As young as I was, I did not understand these profound words, but somehow I felt the weight of their importance and caught the contagious national pride of being a child of a truly independent country. I was a patriot (I did not know the meaning of the word) ready to serve my country (however that was possible).

Our teachers were very serious about making sure that students respected the white and green flag as it was hoisted for the assembly and the singing of the anthem. We were to stand at attention, showing respect, and any mischief-makers would receive the stern look of a displeased teacher.

The Nigerian national anthem was important at home too. My parents, during their childhood in the 1940s, did not have the privilege of experiencing such national pride and self-respect because Nigeria was a British colony then, during the reign of King George VI, the father and predecessor of Queen Elizabeth II. At school, as the Union Jack was hoisted, they sang "God Save the King":

God save our gracious King.
Long live our noble King.
God save the King.
Send him victories,
Happy and glorious,
Long to reign over us,
God save the King.

O Lord our God, arise,
Scatter his enemies
And make them fall;

Confound their politics,
Frustrate their knavish tricks,
On thee our hope we fix,
God save us all!

Quite the contrast from what I was taught. My guess is
that the African students in British colonies, who sang this
song every day at school, could not even imagine that their
own children would sing allegiance to their own country
and their own national aspirations.

My parents accept as a historical fact that from a very
young age they were taught to submit to the British mon-
archy. They believed themselves to be the subjects of King
George VI without any bitterness, rancor, or resistance.
They were not slaves, after all; they were freeborn Africans. They enjoyed the rights and freedoms accorded to
other British subjects. They had their local traditional rulers: the *Ezes* and *Igwes* and *Obas*. Yet their country was
not really theirs, and they were not really free to be their
own people. Colonialism robbed Africans not only of
their natural resources but, even more importantly, of their
self-confidence and their freedom to govern themselves.

We have a common saying in my tribe: "Beke wu
agbara", which translates roughly as "The white man is
spirit." We saw the Europeans as powerful spirits, super-
human masters who were superior to us and therefore
entitled to exercise authority over us. With little or no
resistance on the part of Africans, they made decisions for
tribes across the entire continent of Africa.

The Scramble for Africa

By the mid-nineteenth century, the European powers considered Africa ripe for exploration, trade, and settlement.

They convened the Berlin Conference of 1884–1885 to partition Africa into territories that would then be occupied, annexed, and colonized by the participating countries. The conference ushered in a period of heightened colonial activity by Europeans, which eliminated or overrode most existing forms of African governance.

Kevin Shillington explained the onset of this scramble in his book *History of Africa*: "Subsaharan Africa, one of the last regions of the world largely untouched by 'informal imperialism', was attractive to Europe's ruling elites for economic, political and social reasons." One of those economic reasons, according to Shillington, was the growing trade deficit in Europe. "Africa offered Britain, Germany, France and other countries an open market that would garner them a trade surplus: a market that bought more from the colonial power than it sold overall."[1] In addition, European surplus capital was often more profitably invested overseas, where cheap materials and labor and abundant raw materials lowered manufacturing costs.

Here is a list of African countries alongside their colonial rulers (except Liberia, which was a colony of America).

Algeria	France
Angola	Portugal
Benin	France
Botswana	Britain
Burkina Faso	France
Burundi	Belgium
Cameroon	France-administered UN trusteeship

---

[1] Kevin Shillington, *History of Africa*, rev. 2nd ed. (New York: Macmillan, 2005), p. 301.

Cape Verde	Portugal
Central African Republic	France
Chad	France
Comoros	France
Congo-Brazzaville	France
Côte d'Ivoire	France
Democratic Republic of the Congo	Belgium
Djibouti	France
Egypt	Britain
Equatorial Guinea	Spain
Eritrea	Italy
Ethiopia	—
Gabon	France
The Gambia	Britain
Ghana	Britain
Guinea	France
Guinea-Bissau	Portugal
Kenya	Britain
Lesotho	Britain
Liberia	American Colonization Society
Libya	Italy
Madagascar	France
Malawi	Britain
Mali	France
Mauritania	France
Mauritius	Britain
Morocco	France
Mozambique	Portugal
Namibia	South African mandate
Niger	France
Nigeria	Britain

Rwanda	Belgium-administered UN trusteeship
São Tomé and Príncipe	Portugal
Senegal	France
Seychelles	Britain
Sierra Leone	Britain
British Somaliland	Britain
Italian Somaliland	Italy
South Africa	Britain
Sudan	Britain
Swaziland	Britain
Tanzania	Britain
Togo	France-administered UN trusteeship
Tunisia	France
Uganda	Britain
Zambia	Britain
Zimbabwe	Britain

So, in the scramble for Africa, Britain got nineteen countries, France twenty, Portugal five, Belgium three, and Italy three. The American Colonization Society, Spain, and South Africa each got one. Ethiopia was the only African country that was not colonized.

The Decolonization of Africa

In February 1941, United States President Franklin D. Roosevelt and British Prime Minister Winston Churchill met to discuss their vision for the post–World War II world. The result was the Atlantic Charter, issued the following August, which contained eight principles agreed upon by the two leaders. The following are three of them:

The President of the United States and the Prime Minister, Mr. Churchill, representing H. M. Government in the United Kingdom, being met together, deem it right to make known certain common principles in the national policies of their respective countries on which they base their hopes for a better future for the world.

1. Their countries seek no aggrandissement, territorial or other.
2. They desire to see no territorial changes that do not accord with the freely expressed wishes of the peoples concerned.
3. They respect the right of all peoples to choose the form of Government under which they will live; and they wish to see sovereign rights and self-government restored to those who have been forcibly deprived of them.[2]

In naming self-government as "the right of all peoples", the Atlantic Charter called for the autonomy of the imperial colonies. After World War II ended in 1945, the United States began to pressure Britain to abide by the terms of the Atlantic Charter, and the political will to end colonization grew among Africans. Their leaders arose and led the courageous campaign to decolonize their countries. Among these were the renowned nationalists Kwame Nkrumah of Ghana, Jomo Kenyatta of Kenya, Julius Nyerere of Tanzania, Nnamdi Azikiwe of Nigeria, Ahmed Sékou Touré of Guinea, and Félix Houphouët-Boigny of Côte d'Ivoire.

At the end of the 1950s, African nations started gaining independence, one after another. Africans started to write

[2] Atlantic Charter: Declaration of Principles Issued by the President of the United States and the Prime Minister of the United Kingdom, August 14, 1941, NATO, http://www.nato.int/cps/en/natohq/official_texts_16912.htm.

their own history on the sands of time as they became the protagonists of their own story. From then on it was up to them to make or break their own political, economic, educational, social, judicial, and health systems. Anyone who has followed the journey of these independent African nations in the past fifty years will know that decolonization has not been easy; far from it. There have been many afflictions and much friction brought about by a number of complex factors, including corruption in high places, greed at all levels, and natural and unnatural disasters. Many would describe postcolonial Africa as a poor and plagued continent. But as the late Ahmed Sékou Touré of Guinea famously said to the French general Charles de Gaulle: "We prefer poverty in liberty to riches in slavery."[3]

African Postcolonial Relations

There are still links between the developing independent countries of Africa and the developed Western world. It might be too simplistic, though not necessarily inaccurate, to say that some African countries still have an umbilical cord connecting them directly to their former colonial masters, as can be seen in the French foreign policy of Françafrique and in the Commonwealth of Nations (formerly the British Commonwealth), which Nigeria joined in 1960.

Brian Eads wrote about Françafrique, the relationship between France and its former African colonies, in the

---

[3] Mawuna Koutonin, "14 African Countries Forced by France to Pay Colonial Tax for the Benefits of Slavery and Colonization", Silicon Africa, January 28, 2014, http://siliconafrica.com/france-colonial-tax/.

Newsweek article "France Is Slowly Reclaiming Its Old African Empire".[4] He explains that in the late 1950s, President Charles de Gaulle adopted a plan to maintain ties with two dozen countries in France's former African empire. France had several reasons for this plan, including needed natural resources (one-quarter of its electricity is generated with uranium from Niger). According to Eads, the policy has been carried out under the authority of the French president through its "African cell", which "operated in the shadows, via personal contacts and an undercover network of spies, the military, big business, the Corsican mafia and mercenaries, without parliamentary oversight or approval."

And the result of this ongoing French interference in Africa? "To date, the French have made more than 40 overt military interventions in Africa, often to protect leaders they like and remove those they don't." Needless to say, there is much corruption in these exchanges between African and French leaders. As Eads reported: "Robert Bourgi, a Franco-Lebanese lawyer born in Senegal who was the Élysée Palace's unofficial go-between with African leaders for almost three decades, claims he delivered bags of cash from African leaders to senior French politicians up to and including President Jacques Chirac, who left office in 2007."

In their dealings with developed Western countries, African countries seem to be in a constant posture of respect and deference. Africans appreciate their multitude of highly educated men and women who are achieving great feats in their areas of expertise, but they still

---

[4] Brian Eads, "France Is Slowly Reclaiming Its Old African Empire", *Newsweek*, October 30, 2014, http://www.newsweek.com/2014/11/07/france -slowly-reclaiming-its-old-african-empire-280635.html?amp=1.

subconsciously see European and American experts as the real authorities in their fields. Thus, if an American research organization, such as the Guttmacher Institute, posits that legal abortion will reduce maternal mortality rates, African leaders are likely to heed whatever recommendations they make, even at the cost of eclipsing their own beliefs about abortion. This obedience is due to the African predisposition, from the days of colonialism, to look up to the White Man.

A few years ago, I had a conversation with the speaker of the house of an East African country about an upcoming abortion bill. He was very gracious to me in every way, but he told me without mincing words that the assembly was receiving strong recommendations from European and American experts to legalize abortion. I had seen such deference to these experts many times.

Usually added to the persuasive arguments from Western experts are financial inducements. African nations receive from Europe and America about $43 billion in aid every year, mostly from Western government-aid agencies. This aid often comes with strings attached, as in compliance with population-control measures, including abortion.

Africa Endowed with Treasures

I sometimes think of Africa as an orphaned child who, unbeknownst to himself, has inherited a great deal of wealth and goes about living on meager donations. Africa's first and finest treasure is her people—more than one billion people of diverse tribes and ethnic groups who speak two thousand languages. We have men and women who have attained the highest level of their professions and who continue to strive and thrive even in adverse conditions. Africa has had twenty-two Nobel laureates from nine countries.

In spite of the circulating narrative that African women are overwhelmingly oppressed and enslaved by the chains of patriarchy, since our independence we have seen seven female presidents and twelve female vice presidents in Africa; this is by far a higher proportion of female leadership at the highest levels than on any other continent, even Europe. African women occupy many positions of leadership in public service. Rwanda, for example, has the highest proportion of female parliamentarians in the world—64 percent. The United Kingdom by comparison has only 29 percent.

Africa has much natural beauty—from mountains to jungles and plains; from deserts to lakes and waterfalls. It is also home to a great variety of exotic animals, rare plants, expensive woods, and tropical fruits. Though much of our natural resources are barely harnessed, Africa is endowed with large reserves of diamonds, gold, iron, cobalt, uranium, copper, bauxite, silver, and petroleum.

All this wealth combined with Africa's newfound independence has brought increasing prosperity to many Africans. According to the International Monetary Fund (IMF), half of the fastest growing economies in the world are in Africa. In 2017 the gross national product (GDP) for the West African countries of Côte d'Ivoire and Ghana increased by 7.6 percent and 5.9 percent, respectively, while the average rate of increase in advanced economies was 2.2 percent.[5] Africa also has booming consumer markets; for example, it has become the world's

---

[5] International Monetary Fund, *World Economic Outlook*, October 2017, http://www.imf.org/external/datamapper/NGDP_RPCH@WEO/OEMDC/ADVEC/WEOWORLD.

fastest-growing mobile-phone market. Within the space of five years, the continent's mobile-phone use increased at an annual rate of 65 percent, twice the global average. According to a 2014 survey by the African Development Bank, more than one in three Africans entered the middle class in the past decade, and economists predict that their numbers are set to swell due to rapid economic growth across the continent.[6]

Woe to the Africa in Need

What I have just described is the real but unrecognizable Africa. It is unrecognizable because the Western media rarely shows any good news out of Africa. Instead they show every parameter of failure: low life expectancy, much poverty, poor healthcare quality, high maternal and infant mortality, low food security, little government transparency, and so on. The majority of sub-Saharan African countries score poorly on these indicators. So, on the barometer of wellness, we rank as unwell. On the scale of health, we look underweight and undernourished. On the yardstick of development, we look stunted.

Thus, most of the developed world looks upon us with pity; they see us as "people in need". For many Western celebrities and goodwill ambassadors, Africa remains the favorite destination for humanitarian-aid tourism. HIV-ravaged countries in southern Africa, western African countries decimated by Ebola, drought- and famine-afflicted Ethiopia, refugee-inundated Sudan, war-torn Central Africa—these have become the poster children for

[6]Susan Njanji, "One-Third of Africans Have Entered Middle Class", Yahoo! News, October 27, 2014, https://www.yahoo.com/news/one-three -africans-entered-middle-class-175053335.html.

Africa in need. Yet such images make us vulnerable to the wiles of those who seek to colonize us and to the many African leaders who will readily let them do so in exchange for funds from the West. And by means of this aid, children of independent African nations, like me, have become heavily burdened by the spirit of the colonized.

No wonder, when Melinda Gates launched her extensive contraception projects through the Gates Foundation, African ministers of health signed up for them with alacrity, without even asking about the possible detrimental effects the contraceptive drugs and devices might cause African women. No wonder, when notorious abortion giants such as Marie Stopes International propose questionable projects targeting vulnerable women and girls in Africa, they get incredible numbers of partners who refuse to see the organization's record number of scandals in Great Britain. No wonder, when any number of Western self-proclaimed experts tell our leaders that the most important aspect of development is reproductive rights, our leaders nod in agreement because of the money tied so tightly to this condom campaign or that "safe abortion" bill.

In many ways, it seems as if African nations have gone into a mental condition of "protected dependency" and have thereby put themselves at risk of becoming once again protectorate states of Western stakeholders. This is the path to the past, and the path to perdition.

Aid to the Africa in Need: The Door to Ideological Colonialism

When I was about eight years old, I learned the soulful 1985 single "We Are the World". Back then in our little town, this song was played at every birthday party and even

at wedding receptions. My friends at my all-girls boarding
school and I would play it full blast during our end-of-year
party, to the chagrin of our teachers. We would sing it with
gusto and do our best Michael Jackson, Stevie Wonder,
Lionel Richie, Kenny Rogers, Tina Turner, and Diana
Ross impersonations. Here are the most familiar lyrics:

> We are the world, we are the children
> We are the ones who make a brighter day
> So let's start giving
> There's a choice we're making
> We're saving our own lives
> It's true we'll make a better day
> Just you and me[7]

My friends and I thought that this song was about *us*, that
is, about *our* making the world a better place by being
virtuous and generous. We believed that we were "the
children", that we were "the ones" to make the world
brighter with our love. We did not know that the song
was about the misery of us little African children, about
our poverty, our wretchedness, our hunger. We did not
know that the "people dying" referred to Africans, and
that these gracious American musicians were calling upon
the rest of the world to save us.

As morally indefensible as colonialism was, there were
many in Europe in the 1890s who believed that colonization was, in fact, for the benefit of the people they colonized. This sentiment that has since been aptly described
as philanthropic racism was captured in Rudyard Kipling's
1899 poem "The White Man's Burden".

---

[7] Michael Jackson and Lionel Richie, "We Are the World", © 1985 by
Sony/ATV Music Publishing LLC, Warner/Chappell Music, Inc.

Take up the White Man's burden—
Send forth the best ye breed—
Go bind your sons to exile
To serve your captives' need;
To wait in heavy harness
On fluttered folk and wild—
Your new-caught sullen peoples,
Half devil and half child.

Take up the White Man's burden—
In patience to abide
To veil the threat of terror
And check the show of pride;
By open speech and simple,
An hundred times made plain,
To seek another's profit,
And work another's gain.

Take up the White Man's burden—
The savage wars of peace—
Fill full the mouth of famine
And bid the sickness cease;
And when your goal is nearest
The end for others sought,
Watch Sloth and heathen Folly
Bring all your hopes to nought.

This poem was well received in many quarters, and its author won a Nobel Prize in Literature in 1907, at the age of forty-two, making him the first English-language writer to receive the prize and its youngest recipient to date.

Fast-forward to July 2012, when the British government decided to increase the percentage of its international aid budget dedicated to family planning (contraceptive drugs and devices) in Africa and other parts of the developing world. The government, in explaining its decision to other donor countries, stated: "Family planning is excellent value for money. Every £1 spent on family planning can save governments nearly £6 on healthcare spending, housing, water and other public services."[8] This statement has unfortunately been recycled many times by wealthy Western donors who, in their aid to Africa, are looking for "value for money". Their family-planning programs are the twenty-first-century version of philanthropic racism, in which Africa is considered the "burden" of the donor countries (or dare I say, colonizing countries), who are most interested in spending less by reducing the populations they see themselves as serving.

The United States Agency for International Development (USAID) makes a similar statement regarding their achievements in "family planning priority countries", which are mostly African:

> In USAID's 24 family planning priority countries, the average number of children per woman has decreased from about 5 in 2000 to 4 in 2017, and the percentage of women in these countries using a modern method of contraception has increased from 18 percent to 36 percent over the same time period. In addition to wide-ranging economic and health benefits, family planning is a cost-effective investment.[9]

All of these donors claim to have Africa's best interests at heart. To persuade others of the rightness of their

---

[8] "Family Planning: UK Aid Saves a Woman's Life Every Two Hours", GOV.UK, July 11, 2012, https://www.gov.uk/government/news/family-planning-uk-aid-saves-a-woman-s-life-every-two-hours.

[9] "Population Policies and Reproductive Health", fiscal year 2014, USAID, https://results.usaid.gov/results/sector/population-policies-and-reproductive-health?fiscalYear=2014.

family-planning crusade they use statements such as the
following:

- Contraception is the key to unlocking the economic
  potential of the African woman.
- Legal abortion will reduce maternal mortality in
  Africa.
- Condoms will eradicate a sexually transmitted disease
  epidemic.
- Same-sex marriage is the measure of equality in any
  society.
- Young people should "empowered" with compre-
  hensive sexuality education.
- The traditional family structure of father, mother, and
  children is oppressive.

Yet these statements are diametrically opposed to Africans'
prevalent cultural beliefs and, as I will show, are ultimately
destructive of our people.

Africans by and large believe that sex is sacred, that
human life is precious from womb to tomb, that children
are blessings, that motherhood is desirable, and that marriage between man and woman is life-generating. These
are the basic family values that our parents and grandparents transmitted to us. They are embedded in our customs,
enshrined in our laws, and even encoded in our native languages. To take them away from us amounts to invasion,
occupation, annexation, and colonization of our people.

There is a new colonialism in our time—not of lands
or of natural resources but of the heart, mind, and soul of
Africa. It is an ideological colonialism.

I

Population Control

Population-Explosion Alarmism

The United Nations Department of Economic and Social
Affairs (UN DESA) has projected Africa's share of global
population to grow to 25 percent in 2050 and to 39 percent in 2100.[1] Much of this growth would be the result of
the phenomenal fertility of women in sub-Saharan Africa.
This population boom could, under the right conditions,
form the base of a formidable workforce and tax base
that, if well managed and leveraged, could make Africa
the world's largest market and a dominant player in the
global economy.

On the other hand, the same forecast shows that, from
2010 through 2015, eighty-three countries, including
some of the most powerful nations in the world—China,
Germany, and Russia—had below-replacement fertility.[2]
Yet the most publicized Western demographers, and the
policy leaders who listen to them, have chosen to sound
the alarm with their vision of an African population bomb

[1] United Nations Department of Economic and Social Affairs, Population
Division, *World Population Prospects: The 2015 Revision, Key Findings and Advance
Tables* (New York: United Nations, 2015), p. 3, https://esa.un.org/unpd
/wpp/Publications/Files/Key_Findings_WPP_2015.pdf.
[2] Ibid., p. 10.

instead of a population *boom*, which could help to grow African economies and to lift many Africans out of poverty. They are instilling fear in African leaders by painting a vivid picture of their countries at the sharp edge of environmental destruction, natural-resource depletion, hunger, poverty, pandemic, and disorder. In their narration of the fate of Africa, they bring back to life every debunked Malthusian prediction.

Malthusian scholars and thinkers, such as Paul Ehrlich, renowned author of the 1968 book *The Population Bomb*, are still consulted for their thoughts and recommendations regarding world demographics, particularly in Africa, and their opinions resound in the statements of leading scholars on the issue. In an article about the high birth rate in Niger, John May, with the Population Reference Bureau, was quoted as saying: "This is a time bomb, because all the Sahel is in this situation, and especially with climate change, the food supply will be less abundant than before. It's a huge crisis."[3] It is with this Malthusian mind-set that solutions are being formed and proposed for Africa.

These solutions rely heavily on a single-minded strategy that entails removing or drastically reducing the source of the population growth in Africa—female fertility. Thus, Western nations, organizations, and foundations wage war against the bodies of African women. The first weapon in their arsenal is contraceptive drugs and devices, usually referred to as "family planning". According to the UN DESA: "To realize the substantial reductions in fertility

[3] Quoted in Jill Filipovic, "Why Have Four Children When You Could Have Seven? Family Planning in Niger", *Guardian*, March 15, 2017, https://www.theguardian.com/global-development-professionals-network/2017/mar/15/why-have-four-children-when-you-could-have-seven-contraception-niger?CMP.

projected in medium variant, it is essential to invest in reproductive health and family planning, particularly in the least developed countries."[4] Jagdish Upadhyay, an executive at the United Nations Population Fund (UNFPA), described contraception as a human right: "If all actors can work together to provide women in every country with the means, which is their right, to voluntarily exercise yet another right to freely determine their family size, then we are likely to see a significant slowing of global population growth."[5]

An interview with a well-known British television personality published in the *Telegraph* in 2013 displays this population-explosion alarmism.[6] Unless more population-control efforts are made, he said, the world is "heading for disaster". Also evident in the interview is the Englishman's condescension toward the people of Africa and his lack of understanding of the situation in Africa. Many of his comments were predicated on falsehoods and prejudices, not on facts. For example, he stated that the famines in Ethiopia are caused by too many people living on too little land. Yet the population density of Ethiopia is 82.6 per square kilometer, whereas the population density of Great Britain is 302 per square kilometer. With more than three times the population density of Ethiopia, Britain has more than enough food to feed its population. So how can anyone living there

[4] United Nations Department of Economic and Social Affairs, *World Population Prospects*, p. 5.

[5] Quoted in Liz Ford, "Rise in Use of Contraception Offers Hope for Containing Global Population", *Guardian*, March 8, 2016, https://www.theguardian.com/global-development/2016/mar/08/rise-use-contraception-global-population-growth-family-planning.

[6] Quoted in Hannah Furness, "If We Do Not Control the Population the Natural World Will", *Telegraph*, September 18, 2013, http://www.telegraph.co.uk/culture/tvandradio/10316271/Sir-David-Attenborough-If-we-do-not-control-population-the-natural-world-will.html.

tell the Ethiopians to control their "wild" reproduction rate or forever face the scourge of famine? The reporter did not ask questions along these lines, of course, but simply passed along the Englishman's ominous warning that if we do not act soon, with greater population-control efforts, "the natural world will do something."

The Englishman's view is neither new nor fresh; it is the same theory that many before him have promoted— the theory of the bogus menace of the ticking population time bomb, which is bound to explode if the fertility rate in the developing world is not reduced right away.

According to many experts, a big problem in much of the world is not that too many people are being born but that too few are. For them, the concern is not a population explosion brought on by high birth rates but a population implosion caused by low birth rates. Some are calling the phenomenon a "demographic winter". Science writer Fred Pearce reported that "half the world's nations have fertility rates below replacement level, of just over two children per woman. Countries across Europe and the Far East are teetering on a demographic cliff, with rates below 1.5. On recent trends, Germany and Italy could see their populations halved within the next 60 years." He added that "many demographers expect a global crash to be under way by 2076."[7]

The demographic decline now occurring in developed countries, where the fertility rate has dropped below the replacement rate, is creating all sorts of challenges associated with an aging population: labor shortages, loss of tax

[7] Fred Pearce, "The World in 2076: The Population Bomb Has Imploded", *New Scientist*, November 16, 2016, https://www.newscientist.com/article /mg23231001-400-the-world-in-2076-the-population-bomb-did-go-off-but -were-ok/?utm_campaign=Echobox&utm_medium=Social&utm _source=Twitter#link_time=1499341645).

revenue and the resulting increase in public debt, unsustainable social health and welfare systems, and countless old people without anyone to care for them. A case in point is Japan, "a nation with an unprecedented rapidly aging and declining population".[8] For the past twenty years or so, Japan has been suffering from a declining birth rate and, as a consequence, has seen little or no economic growth.[9] In 2015 about 1 million babies were born, a slight increase over the previous year, but 1.3 million people died, amounting to a net loss of almost 300,000 people.[10]

The shrinking population has adversely affected Japanese society. Many young adults have moved to the cities for jobs, leaving the elderly behind in economically declining towns with fewer and fewer resources and services, including healthcare providers. For this reason, the Japanese government has been attempting to entice working people back to the villages by shoring up lagging fisheries and farms, while trying to figure out ways to relocate some of the elderly to more populous areas. In the effort to reverse the fertility trend, boosting the birth rate has become one of the goals of Prime Minister Shinzō Abe's administration, which has declared that it will raise the fertility rate from the current 1.4 to 1.8 by 2025 or so. The government hopes to encourage more births by making it

[8] "Japan's Depopulation Time Bomb", *Japan Times*, April 17, 2013, http://www.japantimes.co.jp/opinion/2013/04/17/editorials/japans-depopulation-time-bomb/#.WLiZOPnyvIV.

[9] *Economist*, "The Japanese Solution", https://www.economist.com/news/finance-and-economics/21677648-despite-shinzo-abes-best-efforts-japans-economic-future-will-be-leap.

[10] Kyodo, "Slightly More Babies Born Last Year in Japan, but Population Suffers Net Loss of Almost 300,000 People", *Japan Times*, January 1, 2016, https://www.japantimes.co.jp/news/2016/01/01/national/slightly-babies-born-last-year-japan-population-suffers-net-loss-almost-300000-people/#.WbrGXkHTWEd.

easier for families to raise children, such as by increasing the places available in nursery schools.[11]

Although population size is not as much of a concern in Europe and the United States because of immigration, which Japan does not want to increase, these places too are experiencing the so-called graying of their populations. Upside-down family trees, with more elderly people than young people, are commonplace. As a result, the unavoidable fate of many old people is the nursing home, where loneliness, neglect, and even abuse are rampant. In contrast, in the developing world, there are enough children and grandchildren to care for the elderly in warm, loving multigenerational households. For many Africans, children and grandchildren are a sure and steady source of tender loving care in old age, although population-control enthusiasts may see them as nothing more than a sure and steady source of pollution and carbon dioxide emission. Even among the poorest in the developing world, a child is considered not just a mouth to feed but a gift to the family and the community.

With regard to population, Africa's problem has more to do with uncontrolled urbanization. Most African governments invest most of their development funds in a few strategic cities, which has caused mass migration into these areas by people searching for jobs and basic amenities such as electricity, healthcare facilities, and schools. A striking example is Lagos, the commercial center of Nigeria. The megacity of 16 million people is in the smallest state of Nigeria, also called Lagos. The state has less than

[11] Mizuho Aoki, "In Sexless Japan, Almost Half of Single Young Men and Women are Virgins: Survey", *Japan Times*, September 16, 2016, https://www.japantimes.co.jp/news/2016/09/16/national/social-issues/sexless-japan-almost-half-young-men-women-virgins-survey/#.WbrB-EHTWEc.

0.5 percent of the country's landmass, yet 10 percent of the Nigerian population lives in the Lagos metropolitan area, which takes up about a fourth of the state. Lagos has been a magnet because it is the financial center of the country and a major economic hub in West Africa. Similar urban sprawl can be seen in other key African cities such as Douala, Nairobi, and Kampala. Migration to these cities has placed a strain on the existing infrastructure and has resulted in the growth of huge slums, where many people end up when they cannot afford better housing. These slums are usually horrible places with hazardous living conditions. The solution to the slums is not depopulation but rather investment in rural Africa, in its agricultural sector, so that people can make a living wherever they are. If development were more even, severe and unsustainable urbanization would be reduced because people would return to or remain in the regions they are from. Then Africa's growing working-age population would become an economic asset rather than an economic liability.

Ignoring the Desire for Children

For world leaders, the plan of action is very clear—a dedicated effort in population control in developing countries. But in their single-minded obsession to reduce the fertility rate of women in sub-Saharan Africa, the one important consideration the experts have omitted is the desired fertility rate of the women in question.

In 2010, USAID released a report on the number of children desired by people in various parts of the world. It was quite revelatory, as it showed that the desired number of children is highest among people in western and middle Africa, ranging from 4.8 in Ghana to 9.1 in Niger and 9.2 in Chad, with an average of 6.1children for the region.[12] In all the regions and countries surveyed, the level of unwanted births is also remarkably lowest, at 6 percent, in eighteen west and middle African countries. In fact, the report shows that in a country such as Niger, there is hardly any indication of unwanted fertility. In other words, women in Niger consider all their babies as wanted (even when pregnancy is unplanned).[13]

These facts call into question the much-lamented crisis of "unmet need" for family planning. "Unmet need" has become the phrase used within Western elite circles to speak about the "appallingly low" prevalence of contraception use in developing countries. It has become the core of their case for multibillion-dollar contraception projects, the scaffold for their most important policies, and their first and last talking points at every population-themed event. They have even come up with an estimated number of women with unmet need for family-planning services—220 million. They assume that these millions of women fail to contracept because they lack contraceptives, but in reality most of these women desire to have children—in fact, many children. There is a big difference between the invented unmet need and the real unmet needs of African women.

In the article "Why Have Four Children When You Could Have Seven? Family Planning in Niger", Western journalist Jill Filipovic reported on the strong desire for children in Niger:

> Despite having the highest fertility rate in the world, women and men alike in Niger say they want more

---

[12] Charles F. Westhoff, *Desired Number of Children, 2000–2008*, DHS Comparative Reports No. 25 (Calverton, Md.: ICF Macro, 2010), p. 3, http://www.dhsprogram.com/pubs/pdf/CR25/CR25.pdf.

[13] Ibid., p. 21.

children than they actually have—women want an average of nine, while men say they want 11....

Mariama Hassan, who has lived in Darey Maliki village her whole life, got married at 18, late by village standards. As she breastfeeds her daughter, Ramatou, she says she wants to see her baby girl finish school, and eventually get married as well—but not until she's 25. "I want her to be a doctor," Hassan says. "I say 25 because I want her to be mature before getting married, and I want her to finish her studies."

Her hopes for her own life are different. "In my lifetime, I want to have what God decides for me," she says. What does that mean in terms of children? She smiles and laughs. "I hope God gives me 12."[14]

Hassan's sentiments match those of many women in Africa who firmly believe that children are good and precious gifts from God.

I am the sixth child of my parents, and in my childhood I was surrounded (both in my neighborhood and in my school) by children from large families that looked much like mine. And even though we were not wealthy at all, our parents were comfortable in their role of welcoming, raising, feeding, and forming many children. Whether we were planned or unplanned, we were certainly precious to our parents, and it was obvious that they thought of us as God's gifts to them.

Africans are the most philoprogenitive people in the world. This reality is perhaps the single most inconvenient truth behind the resistance to population control in various African communities. It is the unvarnished truth that refutes every fragile project or policy built upon the claim of "unmet need". It is the disruptive truth that population-control experts, ruling elites, and enthusiasts

[14] Filipovic, "Why Have Four Children?"

have chosen to ignore as they wage war against the fertility of African women.

In the town I come from, a new baby is always welcomed with much joy. In fact, we have a special song reserved for births, a sort of "Gloria in Excelsis Deo". The day a baby is born, the entire village celebrates by singing this song, clapping their hands, and dancing. I can say with certainty that Africans love babies.

With all the challenges and the difficulties of life in Africa, there is much to complain about, and Africans, like many other people, lament their problems openly. Throughout my life I have heard people complain of many things, yet I have never heard a woman complain about her baby (born or unborn).

Even with substandard medical care in most places, women are valiant in pregnancy. And once their babies arrive, they gracefully and heroically embrace their maternal responsibilities. I worked for almost five years in a medical setting in Africa, yet I never heard the clinical term "postpartum depression" until I came to live in Europe. The condition might have been underdiagnosed or hidden, but I never witnessed it, even with the relatively high birth rate around me. (I estimate that I had at least one family member or close friend give birth every single month, so I saw at least a dozen new babies per year.) Amidst all our African afflictions and difficulties, amidst all the socioeconomic and political instabilities, our children are always a firm symbol of hope, a promise of life continuing, a reason to strive for a bright future.

The War against Our Fertility

In 2012 I stumbled upon Melinda Gates' plan to collect pledges for almost $5 billion to ensure that the African woman would be less fertile, less encumbered, and, yes, more "liberated". With her incredible wealth she wanted to replace the legacy of an African woman (which is her child) with the legacy of "child-free sex". I was so out-raged that I wrote a public letter to Melinda Gates, which went viral on the Internet and is now posted on the web-page of the Vatican's Pontifical Council for the Laity.[15]

In that letter, I explained to Gates, a Catholic, that many of the sixty-nine countries she was targeting for her con-traceptive campaign had large Catholic populations, with millions of Catholic women of child-bearing age. Unlike Gates and other Catholic women in the developed West-ern world, African Catholic women tend to regard highly Pope Paul VI's encyclical *Humanae vitae*. African women, in all humility, have heard, understood, and accepted the precious words of the prophetic pope. Women with little education and material wealth have embraced what the average *Vogue*- and *Cosmo*-reading woman in the United Sates has refused to understand: that when sex and marriage and children are separated, promiscuity, divorce, abortion, prostitution, and pornography spread as never before. Contraception brings about not greater respect and freedom for women, said Pope Paul VI, but less.

With most African women faithfully practicing and adhering to a faith (mainly Christian or, in some cases, Muslim), there is a high regard for the sexual act as a sacred and private trust between a husband and a wife. The triv-ialization of sex common in the West is simply not an acceptable part of African society, at least not yet. But the moment huge amounts of contraceptive drugs and devices are injected into our society, they will undoubtedly start to erode the sexual ethics that have been woven into our

---

[15] The complete text of "An African Woman's Open Letter to Melinda Gates" can be found in an appendix on page 197.

culture by our faith, not unlike the erosion that befell the Western world after the mass distribution of the birth control pill began in the 1960s.

As we have seen in the West, the easy availability of contraceptives increases sexual promiscuity and infidelity, especially since sex is presented by the promoters of contraception as a casual pleasure sport that can come with no strings—or babies—attached. I shudder to think of the exponential spread of HIV and other STDs in Africa, as men and women with abundant access to contraceptives take up multiple, concurrent sex partners.

And, of course, there are bound to be inconsistencies and failures in the use of these drugs and devices, so naturally, there will be many more unplanned pregnancies as well. How convenient, then, that the West has been pressuring African governments to loosen their abortion laws.

As if this were not enough, I sadly realized that the pro-contraceptive media blitz that will accompany these drugs and devices will not tell Africans the whole truth about them. They will not be told about failure rates, adverse side effects, and the increased risks of cancer and heart disease. They will not be told that promiscuity itself is the leading cause of sexually transmitted diseases, which hormonal contraceptives such as the pill and the patch do nothing to prevent. Given that women in Western societies are left in the dark about these things, the chances that African women will be respected enough to be given all the facts are rather slim. But unlike most Western women, African women tend not to have regular doctor visits; if African women suffer from negative consequences of contraceptive use, they will suffer from them without follow-up care.

In short, I concluded in my letter to Melinda Gates, I saw her billions of dollars as buying Africans not the real

health care that they need but only misery. Needless to
say, my letter did nothing to stop the Gates Foundation's
full-speed-ahead push for contraceptives. Indeed, two
years later, in November 2014, the foundation sponsored
a huge family-planning conference in Abuja, the capital
of Nigeria.

The Abuja Family Planning Conference had immediate
results in my country. A month later, the Federal Ministry
of Health launched its Nigeria Family Planning Blueprint
to raise contraceptive use among Nigerian married women
from 15 to 36 percent.[16] The cost of the program? Six
hundred million dollars. After all, it takes a lot of money
to change the behavior of millions of women. The urgent
reason given for this huge expense, which will require
massive amounts of foreign aid? To avert 1.6 million unintended pregnancies as well as 400,000 infant and 700,000
child deaths by 2018. The conference leaders argued that
increasing contraceptive use is essential for "sustainable
national development and security" for "maternal and
child health and overall quality of life". They also called
for "increased funding commitments for family planning
and a rights-based approach to reproductive health".

The Ministry of Health and those with vested interests
in promoting contraception are perpetuating the cruel
deception that high maternal mortality rates are the result
of high birth rates. It is true that if fewer children were
born in a given year, fewer mothers would die because
of complications during childbirth. Deaths due to childbirth, however, could also be prevented by better health
care. For example, both Maldives and Tanzania have a

---

[16] Nigeria Federal Ministry of Health, *Nigeria Family Planning Blueprint
(Scale-Up Plan)*, October 2014, https://www.healthpolicyproject.com/ns/docs
/CIP_Nigeria.pdf.

contraception prevalence rate of 35 percent. Yet Maldives has a maternal mortality rate of 68, while Tanzania's is 398. Why do so many more Tanzanian women die during and shortly after childbirth? Poor health care. Let's look at another comparison: Ghana has a very low contraception prevalence rate (19 percent), yet it has a lower maternal mortality rate (319) than Zimbabwe's (443), even though Zimbabwe has a high contraception prevalence rate (58 percent).[17]

In other words, the availability of contraception does not necessarily mean that a country has adequate maternity care. What African nations need is not a massive infusion of contraceptives into their communities but a renewed commitment to building up the various branches of the dilapidated healthcare systems across the continent. Imagine if billions of dollars were invested in that!

Congregating in the Mighty Name of Contraception

There are increasing numbers of gatherings around the world for the sole purpose of moving Africa toward the Western standard of low fertility rates and high contraception prevalence. The Gates Foundation has taken a leadership role in this project, which on its surface is about women but at its core is about population control.

In their 2014 Abuja Family Planning Conference, the Gates Foundation was joined by other Western sponsors,

---

[17] Central Intelligence Agency, *The World Factbook* (Washington, D.C.: Central Intelligence Agency, 2017), "Contraceptive Prevalence Rate", https://www.cia.gov/library/publications/the-world-factbook/fields/2258.html; and "Maternal Mortality Rate", https://www.cia.gov/library/publications/the-world-factbook/fields/2223.html.

including Britain's Department for International Development, the United States Agency for International Development (USAID), the MacArthur Foundation, and the United Nations Population Fund (UNFPA). Any one of these organizations could have single-handedly sponsored a conference in any part of the world, but their reason for having it in Nigeria is worth careful examination. Listed alongside these sponsors as the conference's "corporate partners/planning committee" were about twenty-five powerful organizations, some well known in Europe and America for their promotion of contraception and abortion: International Planned Parenthood Federation (IPPF), Marie Stopes International (MSI), Ipas, Pathfinder, and others. Yes, they all gathered in Abuja to nudge and prod Nigeria toward their ideal of family planning.

The term "family planning" is (or should be) self-explanatory. It should mean the planning of one's family. It should point to married couples who have a family to plan. It should be family centered and should connote self-discipline (for every good plan should be undergirded by discipline). Family planning should be a good, healthy, pure, and beautiful concept. A couple, guided by the spirit of openness to love and life, can plan their family together while understanding that any life conceived by their union is a gift of enormous value. Family planning should be natural and healthy for both husband and wife. It should not be destructive or detrimental to the health of soul and body, as is contraception.

Family planning should entail much love, understanding, generosity of spirit, humility, patience, self-control, fidelity, communication, care, and cooperation. All of these enrich the marital bond and strengthen the family-oriented culture of Nigeria. However, the family-planning conference in Abuja had very little, if anything, to do with self-control or fidelity or patience or even marriage! On the contrary, it promoted a hedonistic, individualistic, selfish view of sex.

In spite of the government's stated goal to focus attention on married women, the conference focused on normalizing sexual activities among Nigerian youth outside of marriage. The conference included highly eroticized campaigns targeting the young and presentations on topics such as "Addressing the Family Planning Service Needs of Youth". What need do youth have for family planning? What is so dire about the family-planning needs of our adolescents to warrant eleven powerful sponsors and twenty-five corporate partners?

The truth is, the listed organizers, sponsors, and planners of this conference are very much in tune with the goals of Family Planning 2020, which, in its own words, "generated global commitments to make high-quality, voluntary family-planning services, information, and supplies more available, acceptable, and affordable for an additional 120 million women and girls in the world's poorest countries by 2020".[18] These wealthy, prestigious organizations gathered in our capital with their conference in order to disparage our widely held cultural and religious views on life, love, marriage, and family. Their campaigns represented nothing less than an attack on the natural modesty and innocence of our vulnerable and impressionable young people.

This conference was not convened out of great necessity in our country, and it was not conceived in Nigeria. Rather, it was convened at the behest of the cultural imperialists who consider themselves our "betters". It

[18] "Overview", Health Policy Project, http://www.familyplanning2020 .org/.

was conceived in the hearts of powerful Western interests who are committed to and profit from spreading the sexual revolution, in spite of the fact that it has resulted in higher-than-ever rates of divorce, illegitimacy, abortion, and STDs in the nations where it originated. They are the same people who are promoting abortion throughout the world. They are the same ones who are pushing the movement to normalize lesbian, gay, bisexual, and transgender (LGBT) identity and behavior. They are the same ones implicated in various draconian population-control programs around the globe in the name of saving the world. And they favor more long-acting contraceptive methods yet are deafeningly silent about the significant medical side effects associated with some, if not all, of these drugs. These have, in many documented cases, proved detrimental and dangerous to women's health and well-being.

The Dangers Undisclosed

Blood clots, sinusitis, nausea, migraines, cardiovascular diseases (notably stroke and heart attack), ovarian cysts, heavier periods, depression, anxiety, weight gain, hair loss, uterine perforation, pelvic inflammatory disease, osteoporosis, breast cancer, and death are among the side effects disclosed by pharmaceutical manufacturers in the fine-print inserts that come with the most familiar contraceptive drugs and devices—oral contraceptives, NuvaRing, intrauterine devices, implants, and injectables. Yet these side effects are rarely discussed by the promoters of contraception or even by the doctors who prescribe them.

When Norplant made its market debut in 1992, it was hailed as a breakthrough for women: they could have a

mere ten-minute procedure to insert the contraceptive
and then not worry about getting pregnant for years.
Because of Norplant's adverse side effects, however, it was
withdrawn from the United Kingdom in 1999. Also in
1999, after years of litigation in the United States, Norplant's manufacturer offered cash settlements to thirty-six
thousand American women who claimed that the drug
had caused side effects that they had not been adequately
warned about, such as excessive menstrual bleeding,
headaches, nausea, dizziness, and depression. The parent
company, American Home Products, offered each of the
plaintiffs $1,500. Three years later, Norplant distribution
ended in the United States.[19]

The distribution of Norplant was not discontinued
globally until 2008, after it had been widely administered
to women in a number of African countries: Egypt, Ghana,
Kenya, Nigeria, Zambia, Zaire (now the Democratic
Republic of the Congo), Rwanda, Malawi, Madagascar,
Tanzania, South Africa, Zimbabwe, and Burkina Faso.[20]
Surely at least some African women have experienced
adverse side effects, but they will likely never receive any
compensation for their suffering, because there will likely
be no class action suit filed on their behalf.

In a more recent case, nearly twenty thousand lawsuits have been filed in the United States against Bayer for
alleged harm done by their Yaz and Yasmin birth control pills. The plaintiffs are seeking both compensatory and

[19] David J. Morrow, "Maker of Norplant Offers a Settlement in Suit
over Effects", *New York Times*, August 27, 1999, https://nytimes.com/1999
/08/27/us/maker-of-norplant-offers-a-settlement-in-suit-over-effects.html
?pagewanted=all&referer=.

[20] Irving Sivin, Harold Nash, and Sandra Waldman, *Jadelle Levonorgestrel,
Rod Implants: A Summary of Scientific Data and Lessons Learned from Programmatic
Experience* (New York: Population Council, 2002), p. 5, http://www.respond
-project.org/pages/files/4_result_areas/Result_1_Global_Learning/LA_PM
_CoP/june2009-launch/Jadelle-Levonorgestrel-Rod-Implants.pdf.

punitive damages for blood clots, heart attacks, strokes, and gall bladder injuries. Some of these potential side effects have been linked with one hundred deaths. The suits claim that Bayer failed to heed warnings about the dangers posed by the synthetic hormone drospirenone, an active ingredient in the pills, and to disclose the information to the public. Bayer says that the hormone is safe and continues to sell Yaz and Yasmin, although the company has already settled thousands of cases for billions of dollars and as of 2017 was expecting further lawsuits. Legal challenges are cropping up in other countries as well. [21]

Several years ago, critics began urging the United States Food and Drug Administration (FDA) to recall birth control pills with drospirenone, and in 2012 the FDA issued the following safety announcement:

The U.S. Food and Drug Administration (FDA) has completed its review of recent observational (epidemiologic) studies regarding the risk of blood clots in women taking drospirenone-containing birth control pills. Drospirenone is a synthetic version of the female hormone, progesterone, also referred to as a progestin. Based on this review, FDA has concluded that drospirenone-containing birth control pills may be associated with a higher risk for blood clots than other progestin-containing pills. FDA is adding information about the studies to the labels of drospirenone-containing birth control pills.[22]

The notification came on the heels of some scientific studies that demonstrated a sixfold increased risk of blood clots in

[21] "Yaz Lawsuits and Litigation", Drugwatch, https://www.drugwatch.com/yaz/lawsuits/.

[22] "FDA Drug Safety Communication: Updated Information about the Risk of Blood Clots in Women Taking Birth Control Pills Containing Drospirenone", U.S. Food and Drug Administration, April 10, 2012, https://www.fda.gov/Drugs/DrugSafety/ucm299305.htm.

users of combined pills with desogestrel, gestodene, drospirenone, or cyproterone acetate, compared with nonusers.[23]

Given the limited reporting on the adverse side effects
of oral contraceptives and the assurances from medical
professionals and pharmaceutical companies that their
benefits outweigh their risks, the global distribution of
the more dangerous pills is not exactly clear. Africa has
been flooded in recent years with various oral contraceptives. In 2014 alone, 77,225,741 units of unspecified birth
control pills were collectively donated to African countries by the UNFPA, USAID, the IPPF, MSI, Population
Services International, the German-government development bank Kreditanstalt für Wiederaufbau, and the British Department for International Development.[24] African
healthcare providers and leaders must find out which pills
are being distributed and what their side effects could be
and then share this information with African women.

Another Bayer contraceptive that has recently stirred
controversy is Essure, a nonsurgical, permanent method of
sterilizing women. It involves inserting tiny coils into the
fallopian tubes. Tissue then builds up around the coils and
blocks sperm from reaching eggs. Essure was hailed as an
affordable, less-invasive alternative to surgical sterilization
procedures that block, cut, or seal the fallopian tubes.[25]

[23] Ø. Lidegaard et al., "Hormonal Contraception and Venous Thrombo-
embolism", *Acta Obstetricia et Gynecologica Scandinavica* 91, no. 7 (July 2012):
769–78.

[24] Dr. Kabir Ahmed et al., *Contraceptives and Condoms for Family Planning
and STI and HIV Prevention: External Procurement Support Report 2014* (New
York: UNFPA, 2014), pp. 102–3, http://www.unfpa.org/sites/default/files
/pub-pdf/UNFPA_External_Procurement_Support_Report.pdf.

[25] Julie Deardorff, "Women Report Complications from Essure Birth Control", *Chicago Tribune*, December 22, 2013, http://articles.chicagotribune.com
/2013-12-22/health/ct-essure-safety-met-20131222_1_essure-conceptus
-fallopian-tubes.

Beginning around 2013, however, the FDA began receiving many adverse-event reports related to this device:

> Reported adverse events include persistent pain, perforation of the uterus and/or fallopian tubes, intra-abdominal or pelvic device migration, abnormal or irregular bleeding, and allergy or hypersensitivity reactions. Some women have had surgical procedures to remove the device. In addition, Essure failure, and, in some cases, incomplete patient follow-up, have resulted in unintended pregnancies.[26]

In 2015 the FDA consulted with doctors and patients about Essure, issued some statements about the possible need for labeling changes, and continued its approval of the product. That same year, an important study of Essure was published by the *BMJ* (formerly *British Medical Journal*). It found that this form of sterilization carried a more than tenfold higher risk of reoperation than laparoscopic sterilization.[27]

The following year, the FDA decided that Essure labeling should henceforth include the addition of the following boxed warning:

> WARNING: Some patients implanted with the Essure System for Permanent Birth Control have experienced and/or reported adverse events, including perforation of the uterus and/or fallopian tubes, identification of inserts in the abdominal or pelvic cavity, persistent pain, and

---

[26] "Essure Permanent Birth Control", U.S. Food and Drug Administration, last modified August 23, 2017, https://www.fda.gov/MedicalDevices/Products andMedicalProcedures/ImplantsandProsthetics/EssurePermanentBirth Control/default.htm.

[27] Jialin Mao et al., "Safety and Efficacy of Hysteroscopic Sterilization Compared with Laparoscopic Sterilization: An Observational Cohort Study", *BMJ* 351 (October 13, 2015), http://www.bmj.com/content/351/bmj.h5162.

suspected allergic or hypersensitivity reactions. If the device needs to be removed to address such an adverse event, a surgical procedure will be required. This information should be shared with patients considering sterilization with the Essure System for Permanent Birth Control during discussion of the benefits and risks of the device.[28]

Bayer complied with the decision and added the FDA warning to its product.[29]

Women claiming to have been harmed by Essure cannot sue Bayer because of a law that indemnifies manufacturers of medical devices. But thousands of them have joined support groups on social media to discuss the debilitating side effects and the baffling medical problems that they have associated with Essure. In 2014 the famous consumer-rights advocate Erin Brockovich, whom Julia Roberts played in an Oscar-winning film, began championing their efforts to convince Bayer to stop manufacturing Essure. In response, Bayer Healthcare, which purchased Essure manufacturer Conceptus in 2013, said that the device was "overwhelmingly safe" and had been placed in 750,000 women worldwide.[30]

WomanCare Global announced in 2011 that it was going to distribute Essure in Ghana, Kenya, Mexico, Puerto Rico, and Turkey. According to its press release, which has been deleted from the organization's website

[28] U.S. Food and Drug Administration, *Labeling for Permanent Hysteroscopically-Placed Tubal Implants Intended for Sterilization: Guidance for Industry and Food and Drug Administration Staff*, October 31, 2016, https://www.fda.gov/downloads/MedicalDevices/DeviceRegulationandGuidance/GuidanceDocuments/UCM488020.pdf.

[29] See Essure website: http://www.essure.com./.

[30] Regan Morris, "Erin Brockovich Calls for End to Bayer's Essure", BBC News, June 24, 2014, http://www.bbc.co.uk/news/business-27871265.

but is published elsewhere, additional countries will be added.[31] Who will advocate for the women in these countries if they experience negative side effects from Essure?

Although American women with grievances against pharmaceutical companies can take action through appeals to the FDA, the media, and the judicial system, the typical African woman has no such means of recourse if she suffers adverse effects from the contraceptives she is being pressured to use. Between the launch of Melinda Gates' contraception campaign in 2012 and 2016, there were 30.2 million additional users of contraception in the "focus countries",[32] and 13 million of these were in Africa.[33]

The contraceptive that has been most assiduously pushed among African populations recently is injectable depot medroxyprogesterone acetate (DMPA), which is commonly known as Depo Provera or simply the Depo shot. The latest form of this shot can be administered under the skin (subcutaneously) once every three months. A 2014 UNFPA report recommended the use of DMPA in the developing world:

It is hoped that the introduction of sub-cutaneous DMPA will address the unmet need for family planning through: (i) attracting new users; (ii) method switching from traditional and other temporary methods; and (iii) reduction of discontinuation rate of injectable contraceptives. Potential

[31] "WomanCare Global to Distribute Essure in 5 Countries", Reproductive Health Supplies Coalition, January 11, 2011, https://www.rhsupplies .org/news-events/news/article/womancare-global-to-distribute-essure-r-in -5-countries-1283/.

[32] Family Planning 2020, "Additional Users and mCPR", chap. 3 in *FP2020 Momentum at the Midpoint, 2015–2016*, http://progress.familyplanning2020.org /page/measurement/additional-users-mcpr-indicator-1-2.

[33] "Additional Users by Region, 2016", in ibid., http://progress.family planning2020.org/uploads/04/12/Additional_Users_by_Region_900px.png.

advantages of sub-cutaneous DMPA include increased convenience and ease of administration and the potential to contribute to system-level logistics benefits in terms of storage, transport, and distribution.

Sub-cutaneous DMPA is recommended as an addition to the family planning method mix, serving to extend access and increase use in resource-constrained settings, potentially also in humanitarian situations.[34]

According to the same report, as of 2014 Western donor nations and organizations had contributed more than 102 million injectable contraceptives, and 50 percent of them had been given to African countries.

An example of the injectable-birth-control trend is the agreement between Pfizer Inc., the Bill and Melinda Gates Foundation, and the Children's Investment Fund Foundation to expand access to Pfizer's injectable contraceptive, Sayana Press, for women in the world's poorest countries.[35] Some of the countries targeted for contraception injections are Burkina Faso, Kenya, Niger, Senegal, Uganda, and Nigeria. The announcement of this project was immediately picked up and praised by many news agencies in the Western world, including the British Broadcasting Corporation (BBC), which described the shot as the "one dollar contraceptive set to make family planning easier".[36] Easier for whom? For Ugandan, Kenyan, and Nigerian women?

[34] Ahmed et al., *Contraceptives and Condoms*, p. 60.

[35] Pfizer, "Novel Agreement Expands Access to Pfizer's Contraceptive, Sayana® Press, for Women Most in Need in the World's Poorest Countries", press release, November 13, 2014, http://press.pfizer.com/press-release/novel-agreement-expands-access-pfizers-contraceptive-sayana-press-women-most-need-worl.

[36] Jane Dreaper, "The One Dollar Contraceptive Set to Make Family Planning Easier", BBC News, November 16, 2014, http://www.bbc.com/news/health-30026001.

For the multibillionaire foundations spearheading the campaign? Or for the pharmaceutical company that just got a dream deal?

How does practically sterilizing the poorest women in the world give them control over famine, draught, disease, and poverty? It does not make them more educated or more employable. It does not provide food or safe drinking water. It does not make African women happier or more satisfied in their marriages. No. This extensive contraception project will only make them sterile at the cheapest rate possible. This is certainly not what we African women have asked for. It is not the help that our hearts crave amidst the trials and difficulties of Africa. But in a world of shocking cultural imperialism, it is what our "betters" have chosen for us.

What makes the massive exportation of injectable contraception downright insidious is that while it is being pushed on African women, it is being questioned in the developed world after having been shown in various studies to carry dangerous and even lethal side effects.

In October 2011 the *New York Times* published the article "Contraceptive Used in Africa May Double Risk of H.I.V.", based on a cohort study by the prestigious medical research journal *Lancet* that showed that "the risk of HIV-1 acquisition doubled with the use of hormonal contraception, especially the injectable methods."[37] This study was partly funded by the Bill and Melinda Gates Foundation,

[37] Renee Heffron et al., "Use of Hormonal Contraceptives and Risk of HIV-1 Transmission: A Prospective Cohort Study", *Lancet* 12, no. 1 (January 2012): 19–26, http://www.thelancet.com/journals/laninf/article/PIIS1473 -3099(11)70247-X/fulltext#article_upsell. See also Pam Belluck, "Contraceptive Used in Africa May Double Risk of H.I.V.", *New York Times*, October 3, 2011, http://www.nytimes.com/2011/10/04/health/04hiv.html ?pagewanted=all&_r=0.

and yet, following these findings, they still launched this high-risk product in the targeted countries of their choice (Uganda, Kenya, Niger, Nigeria, and many others), where the women may not be able to raise their voices when the lethal effects set in.

In addition to the HIV-related effects of injectable contraception, there is also the doubled risk of breast cancer demonstrated by various studies, such as that done by the Fred Hutchinson Cancer Research Center in Seattle and published by the National Institutes of Health in 2013. The research team found that "recent DMPA use for 12 months or longer was associated with a 2.2-fold increased risk of invasive breast cancer."[38]

Furthermore, this same product has been linked to permanent bone-density loss, and regarding this health issue, Pfizer has had a staggering number of prosecutions, class action lawsuits, and out-of-court settlements with millions of dollars in payouts.[39] As a direct result of these cases, the FDA issued the following compulsory warning for the product Depo Provera:

> Use of Depo-subQ Provera 104 or Depo Provera may cause you to lose calcium stored in your bones. The longer you use Depo Provera, the more calcium you are likely to lose. The calcium may not return completely once you stop using Depo Provera. Loss of calcium may cause weak bones that could increase the risk that your bones might break, especially after menopause. It is not

[38] Christopher I. Li et al., "Effect of Depo-Medroxyprogesterone Acetate on Breast Cancer Risk among Women 20–44 Years of Age", NIH Public Access, April 15, 2012, https://aleteiaen.files.wordpress.com/2014/11/nihms359669.pdf.

[39] "Depo-Provera Birth Control and Osteoporosis", BigClassAction .com, June 27, 2005, https://www.bigclassaction.com/lawsuit/depo_provera _contraceptive_osteoporosis_class_action.php.

known whether your risk of developing osteoporosis may be greater if you are a teenager when you start to use Depo Provera. You should only use Depo Provera long term (more than 2 years) if other methods of birth control are not right for you.

How does a product shown to be flawed, dangerous, and in some cases even lethal become what the BBC refers to as the "contraceptive set to make family planning easier"?

The push for use of DMPA in Africa proves that the Western proponents of population control willfully ignore the glaring reality of the hazardous side effects of contraceptives so that they can impose their views and their dangerous products on Africans. In their campaign, conference, and summit speeches, I have never heard any serious mention of these side effects or of the inadequacy of the healthcare systems in Africa to deal with the health problems that are sure to follow widespread use of injectable contraceptives. The insistence on reducing the population of Africa, no matter what the cost to the Africans themselves, is racism, imperialism, and colonialism disguised as philanthropy.

The Hypersexualization of Youth

In the Great Halls of the United Nations

During the fiftieth session of the United Nations Commission on Population and Development, held in April 2017, I attended a side event sponsored by France called "Sexual and Reproductive Health: Meeting the Needs of Young People". What I saw and heard during this event captures perfectly the theme of this chapter.[1]

Beside the French secretary of international development, who led the discussions, were ministers from Francophone African countries who tried to align themselves perfectly with him on issues related to the sexuality of young people: comprehensive sex education, availability of condoms and other contraceptives, and access to reproductive health services. Instead of speaking in favor of their cultural values and traditional views with respect to sexuality, marriage, and family, the African panelists apologized for their peoples' high fertility rates and low contraceptive-usage rates. They were embarrassed by the major role that parents, tradition, and religion assume in their countries,

---

[1] Government of France, "Sexual and Reproductive Health: Meeting the Needs of Young People" (invitation to April 3, 2017, event), http://www.un.org/en/development/desa/population/commission/pdf/50/sideEvents/flyer_france_3April2017.pdf.

especially with regard to youth. Throughout the event, they gazed admiringly at the French secretary and listened attentively to him as he boasted of how young people in France have unhindered access to the contraceptives of their choice and to abortion. The French shamed the African leaders into accepting resolutions to redefine their people's ideals and aspirations, a dynamic of the neocolonialism at work in many international forums and settings, even in the great halls of the United Nations.

Targeting Children: Comprehensive Sexuality Education

In recent years, sexual-rights activists have shifted a great deal of their efforts toward children, primarily by promoting comprehensive sexuality education (CSE) as an international right mandated by law. If they succeed in this ambitious propaganda project, the next generation will be fully formed in radical sexual ideology.

I have sat through many international events in which some Western nations have boldly attempted to push CSE as a key part of human development. Their description of CSE makes it sound neither offensive nor controversial, because they frame it as a major component of the solutions to some of the most complex problems facing developing countries. With CSE, they say, developing countries will be able to ensure the health and well-being of families, promote gender equality, eliminate stereotyped roles for men and women, empower women, reduce maternal and infant mortality, combat HIV/AIDS, end unsafe abortion practices, lower adolescent pregnancy rates, eradicate violence against women, and even create a democratic and pluralistic polity. The platform of which CSE is part is made to sound like the fulfillment of everyone's dreams.

The vision of human sexuality presented in the widely approved CSE curricula, however, would be considered distorted, disruptive, and objectionable in most African countries. This vision assumes that the main purpose of human sexuality is physical pleasure, as can be seen in the Population Council's *It's All One* curriculum for young people ages fifteen and older (the authors encourage educators who teach children younger than fifteen to draw on its contents). According to the program guidelines, "Public health and rights organizations have issued declarations regarding the rights of all persons to sexual expression. These rights include the right to seek pleasure in the context of safety and of mutual and meaningful consent."[2]

This curriculum might as well be the Western sexual liberationists' official handbook on human sexuality. Its topics include sexual rights, sexual diversity, sexual expression and enjoyment, sexual well-being and advocacy, and gender identity. These are presented from a single pleasure-trumps-all perspective and with the single-minded aim to spread the sexual revolution to young Africans.

The program tells young people: "What feels sexually pleasurable varies by person." It encourages masturbation, homosexual acts, and pornography: "People can experience sexual pleasure by touching themselves or through a shared experience (with someone of the same or the other sex). They can also experience sexual pleasure with no touching at all. Sources of sexual pleasure may include

---

[2] Population Council, *It's All One Curriculum*, vol. 1, *Guidelines for a Unified Approach to Sexuality, Gender, HIV, and Human Rights Education* (New York: Population Council, 2009), p. 97, http://www.popcouncil.org/uploads/pdfs/2011PGY_ItsAllOneGuidelines_en.pdf.

fantasies, words, reading, watching a film, caressing, kissing, or genital contact." It directly teaches children to masturbate: "Touching or stroking oneself (especially one's own genitals) for sexual pleasure is called masturbation.... Masturbation is an important way that people learn about their bodies and sexuality.... Masturbation is a safe sexual behavior. It is neither physically nor mentally harmful."[3]

The program lists the following as rights: negotiating condom use, having sex with a person of the same sex, deciding to become pregnant or to have children, obtaining contraceptive information and services, and procuring an abortion.[4] This list of rights is all the more shocking when one considers that they are supposedly rights for children.

With regard to the prevention of sexually transmitted diseases, the curriculum referred to condoms sixty-six times as sure protection. It mentioned abstinence only two times.

This curriculum is consistent with other CSE materials and publications, including the international guidelines on sexuality education, jointly released in 2009 by the World Health Organization (WHO), the United Nations Educational, Scientific, and Cultural Organization (UNESCO), the United Nations Children's Fund (UNICEF), the United Nations Joint Program for HIV/AIDS (UNAIDS), and the United Nations Population Fund (UNFPA).[5] With this kind of backing, it is no wonder that CSE has made it to the top of the list of rights that the United Nations is attempting to universalize. Were this propaganda to become a universal human right, such an outcome would

[3] Ibid., p. 99.
[4] Ibid., p. 28.
[5] United Nations Educational, Scientific, and Cultural Organization, *International Technical Guidance on Sexuality Education:* An Evidence-Informed Approach for Schools, Teachers and Health Educators, vol. 1, *The Rationality for Sexuality Education* (Paris: UNESCO, 2009), http://unesdoc.unesco.org /images/0018/001832/183281e.pdf.

be the triumph of the loudest and wealthiest ideological activists in the world.

The Force of Bills, Policies, and Political Will in Africa

A 2014 Pew Research Center survey showed that a significant majority of people across Africa have conservative views on abortion, contraception, premarital sex, homosexuality, and divorce.[6] This finding reflects my experience growing up in Nigeria. Africans' views on sexual matters are formed by deep-seated cultural or religious beliefs, which are hindering the progress of the proponents of social change who are trying to introduce modern Western standards of behavior in Africa. Thus, it is not surprising that one of the strategies to bring about radical change is to pressure African leaders and legislators to establish new laws and policies that will impose Western standards on their people.

At various international events, I have heard this strategy described as "political will", a term that, by definition, implies a certain show of force and commitment on the part of leaders to carry through a policy, especially one that is not popular. It is a soft version of totalitarianism invoked by imperialists and sexual liberationists who want to force millions of Africans to let go of their morals. Of course, African laws and policies are the work of African leaders, so I do not lay all the blame on the West, but new laws and policies with respect to sexual behavior originate with Western leaders who want to circumvent African parents in order to indoctrinate their children.

[6] Pew Research Center, "Global Views on Morality" (2013 poll), http://www.pewglobal.org/2014/04/15/global-morality/.

In February 2015, the Kenyan government launched its Global ALL IN campaign against HIV and AIDS in adolescents. This campaign was strongly supported by the UNFPA, UNICEF, the WHO, the Global Fund, UNAIDS, and the United States government, all of whom made substantial financial commitments to fund the program.[7] The program sounded good at first, but when its details were finally revealed to the public, it sparked quite a controversy in Kenya, where it became known as the "Condoms for Kids" campaign.[8] By June of that year, a controversial bill that would allow children to receive condoms and birth control pills without parental knowledge or consent was introduced to the Kenyan Parliament.[9]

By 2017, this type of legislative overreach had spread not just to one neighboring country but to the entire region, as the East African Legislative Assembly drafted a bill to distribute contraceptives to children and teenagers between ten and nineteen years old. If passed into law, the "EAC Sexual Reproductive Health and Rights Bill" will require the East African Community member states (Uganda, Kenya, Tanzania, Rwanda, Burundi, and South Sudan) to provide contraceptives to all EAC citizens, including children.[10] The bill was criticized by key leaders

[7] "Global ALL IN Campaign Fights Rising HIV Infections and Deaths among Adolescents", World Health Organization, http://www.afro.who.int /en/kenya/press-materials/item/7378-global-all-in-campaign-fights-rising -hiv-infections-and-deaths-among-adolescents.html.

[8] http://africanspotlight.com/2015/02/18/kenya-president-kenyatta -launches-condoms-kids-campaign/.

[9] Gideon Keter, "Bill to Give Children Condoms, Birth Control without Parent's Approval Pass 2nd Reading", Star, June 25, 2015, http://www.the -star.co.ke/news/2015/06/25/bill-to-give-children-condoms-birth-control -without-parents-approval_c1158462.

[10] Emmanuel Ainebyoona, "East Africa: EALA Bill to Introduce Contra- ceptives for Children", Monitor, March 2, 2017, http://allafrica.com/stories /201703020360.html.

in East Africa, including Dr. Monica Kizito, a Ugandan doctor and a mother who described it as an attack on the family. Yet proponents stand by the bill, as it aligns East Africa with much of the Western world, which already gives children access to contraception, and even abortion, without parental knowledge or consent.

Africa Ravaged by HIV

Since the beginning of the AIDS epidemic, more than 70 million people have been infected with the virus (HIV) that causes the disease, and about 35 million people have died of it. Globally, about 36.7 million people were living with HIV at the end of 2015. Almost 70 percent of these were in sub-Saharan Africa.[11]

Although HIV transmissions have decreased globally since the epidemic reached its peak in the 1990s, the rate at which the virus continues to spread has plateaued. The annual global death toll from AIDS is 1.1 million, and more than 70 percent of those who die from the disease each year are in Africa.[12] So, regardless of what people think, AIDS has claimed and is still claiming too many precious lives across the world, particularly in Africa. Africans especially ought to be asking why this virus has not been stopped in their countries.

Even though gripping documentaries are no longer being made to highlight the epidemic, each year more

[11] "Global Health Observatory (GHO) Data", World Health Organization, http://www.who.int/gho/hiv/en/. UNAIDS, "Fact Sheet 2016: Global Statistics—2015", p. 5, http://www.unaids.org/sites/default/files/media_asset /20150901_FactSheet_2015_en.pdf.

[12] UNAIDS, *Global Aids Update 2016* (Geneva: UNAIDS, 2016), p. 2, http://www.unaids.org/sites/default/files/media_asset/global-AIDS-update -2016_en.pdf.

than 2 million new HIV infections are reported worldwide, with more than 65 percent of those occurring in
Africa, and this number has remained static since 2010. In
other words, it is not decreasing. In sub-Saharan Africa,
young women (fifteen to twenty-four) accounted for
25 percent of new HIV infections among adults, while
women as a whole accounted for 56 percent of new
HIV infections among adults.[13] These are sobering statistics that go beyond numbers into the reality of millions
of people.

What is particularly disturbing about this trend is that
mother-to-child transmission of AIDS is still a big problem
in Africa. How can that be slowed when so many women
of childbearing age are still becoming infected? According to health experts and organizations, the answer to this
plague is to distribute more condoms.

South Africa is praised as a role model in this context,
for it built the world's largest condom program in just a
few years and doubled the number of condoms distributed per male per year in at least seven of nine provinces.
Yet South Africa is among the African countries with the
highest incidence rates of HIV, and it has the highest percentage of HIV-infected young women in southern and
eastern Africa.[14]

I had a series of interesting e-mail correspondences with
a wonderful South African man over humanitarian aid and
foreign intervention in Africa. One of his e-mails to me
was about the tragic failure of the condom agenda in South
Africa to stop the spread of HIV:

---

[13] UNAIDS, *Prevention Gap Report 2016* (Geneva: UNAIDS, 2016), p. 7,
http://www.unaids.org/sites/default/files/media_asset/2016-prevention
-gap-report_en.pdf.

[14] UNAIDS, *Prevention Gap Report*, pp. 8–9.

Dear Uju,

I live in KwaZulu Natal Province in South Africa—
the province with (until recently) the highest rate of HIV
transmission in South Africa, which has the highest rate of
HIV of countries in Africa—and guess what? Every government department and every municipal office has free
condoms everywhere—by the box load! You would think
that people would eventually put 2 and 2 together!

While traditional communities celebrate chastity through
their values and large cultural annual gatherings, the more
"sophisticated" or "educated" are trying to impose their
supposedly "more advanced" agendas, which are contrib-
uting to the breakdown of the most fundamental building
blocks of society—our families!

After reading this, I asked myself: When will the rich
donors listen to Africans? When will they concede
the undeniable failure of their multibillion-dollar condom projects? When will they count the graves of our
people who succumbed to HIV through reckless sexual behavior? And reckless sexual behavior—that is,
promiscuity—is what is ironically promoted through
condom campaigns.

A young Ugandan man told me of his experience as
a freshman in one of the major universities in Uganda.
He went to register with the university health center, as
is recommended for all new students. After he filled out
a medical-history questionnaire, the nurse offered him a
free box of condoms—not vitamins or eye drops or aspi-
rin but condoms. And when the student asked the nurse
why she gave him condoms, she told him that they were
for his protection, part of a larger condom project paid for
by some external stakeholders. He declined the offer and
walked away from the clinic wondering why he was not
told the truth about sex: that the only way to avoid sexually

transmitted diseases is to save sex for a lifelong, monoga-
mous relationship.

The ABCs of Sex

When HIV/AIDS first became an epidemic in Africa,
the ABC prevention plan was developed in response to
it. ABC stands for the following:

Abstinence before marriage
Be faithful in marriage or to one partner
Condom use if A and B are impossible

The A and B approaches were emphasized as the most
effective ways of preventing HIV by completely eliminat-
ing risk. The C approach was understood and accepted as
being the only realistic option for high-risk members of
society (mainly sex workers), whose sexual behavior could
not easily be changed, no matter how much education and
encouragement they might receive.[15]

This ABC program had great success when it was
launched in Uganda, a country with a record-high HIV
infection rate in the general population. The number of
young unmarried people having sex plummeted, and so
did the number of Ugandans reporting multiple partners. An impressive behavior change was seen across the

[15]Edward C. Green, "Establishing Risk Elimination and Improving
Harm Reduction in AIDS Prevention", *Russian Journal of AIDS, Cancer
and Public Health* 13, no. 3 (2009) 46–56, posted on ResearchGate, https://
www.researchgate.net/profile/Edward_Green4/publication/266339129
_Establishing_Risk_Elimination_and_Improving_Harm_Reduction_in
_AIDS_Prevention/links/54c641640cf256ed5a9d8796/Establishing-Risk
-Elimination-and-Improving-Harm-Reduction-in-AIDS-Prevention
.pdf?origin=publication_detail.

country, and in subsequent years, Uganda had the most remarkable reduction in HIV infections ever recorded since the beginning of the AIDS epidemic, as the infection rate dropped by 70 percent.[16] In contrast, in some of the countries with the most extensive condom-distribution networks, the rate of HIV infection remains high.

One would have thought that the great success of the Ugandan initiative would help to shape other prevention programs across Africa, but even with the documented success in Uganda, humanitarian organizations have chosen a different prevention model that does not encourage or require any sexual restraint or responsibility whatsoever. They developed a core prevention message tightly wrapped around the condom, with little, if any, support for the existing abstinence and fidelity programs. Sam Ruteikara, the co-chair of Uganda's National AIDS Prevention Committee, pointed out that his country's original, endogenous, and highly effective behavior-change approach suffered at the expense of the greater promotion of condoms and expensive antiviral drugs, both of which make money for the people who manufacture and distribute them. As a result, the AIDS rate was increasing again:

> In the fight against AIDS, profiteering has trumped prevention. AIDS is no longer simply a disease; it has become a multibillion-dollar industry....
>
> ... [The] international AIDS experts who came to Uganda said we were wrong to try to limit people's sexual freedom. Worse, they had the financial power to force their casual-sex agendas upon us....

[16] Rand L. Stoneburner and Daniel Low-Beer, "Population-Level HIV Declines and Behavioral Risk Avoidance in Uganda", Science 304 (April 30, 2004), http://www.uvm.edu/pdodds/teaching/courses/2009-08UVM-300/docs/others/2004/stoneburner2004.pdf.

So hear my plea, HIV-AIDS profiteers. Let my people
go. We understand that casual sex is dear to you, but stay-
ing alive is dear to us. Listen to African wisdom, and we
will show you how to prevent AIDS.[17]

The Failure to Prevent Death in Africa

Western and international entities such as UNAIDS,
the UNFPA, and the Global Fund claim that their ever-
increasing expenditure on condom campaigns in Africa
is the guaranteed pathway to victory in the battle against
HIV infection—a great obfuscation of the truth that is
costing lives across the continent. According to Edward
Green, former director of the Harvard AIDS Prevention
Project, one of the tragic blunders of modern history is
that even though empirical studies had demonstrated that
Uganda's ABC program was effective, and that condoms
alone would not stop the spread of HIV, condoms and
promiscuity have been promoted while ABC programs
have been discouraged and defunded.[18]

Green is one of the HIV experts who has stumbled upon
the inconvenient truth that condoms, without behavior
change, are not as effective in preventing HIV as proponents claim. In fact, some condom campaigns increase HIV
infection rates because they encourage risky sexual behavior:

In theory, condom promotions ought to work everywhere. And intuitively, some condom use ought to be

[17] Sam L. Ruteikara, "Let My People Go, AIDS Profiteers", *Washington
Post*, June 30, 2008, http://www.washingtonpost.com/wp-dyn/content/article
/2008/06/29/AR2008062901477.html.
[18] Edward Green, *Broken Promises: How the AIDS Establishment Has Betrayed
the Developing World* (Abingdon, U.K.: Routledge, 2011).

better than no use. But that's not what the research in Africa shows.

Why not?

One reason is "risk compensation." That is, when people think they're made safe by using condoms at least some of the time, they actually engage in riskier sex.[19]

The link between condom campaigns and increased risky behavior has been more recently reaffirmed in a study published in 2016 by Kasey Buckles and Daniel Hungerman, economists at the University of Notre Dame. In studying the results of condom-distribution programs in 484 schools over the course of a few years, they estimated that these programs effectively encouraged risky sexual behavior and increased teen fertility by about 10 percent.[20]

"Condomizing" Africa

In spite of the failure rate of condom programs for teenagers, the UNFPA continues to promote its multimillion-dollar campaign across Africa known as CONDOMIZE!, which specifically targets youth, promising them that condom use prevents HIV infection and unwanted pregnancies.[21] Through this campaign Africa is getting more condom donations than ever before. In fact, Africa receives

[19] Edward C. Green, "Condoms, HIV-AIDS, and Africa—The Pope Was Right", *Washington Post*, March 29, 2009, http://www.washingtonpost.com /wp-dyn/content/article/2009/03/27/AR2009032702825.html.

[20] Kasey S. Buckles and Daniel M. Hungerman, *The Incidental Fertility Effects of School Condom Distribution Programs*, University of Notre Dame, May 2016, http://www3.nd.edu/~kbuckles/condoms.pdf.

[21] John Chirwa, "UNFPA Rolls Out a National Condomize Campaign", *Nation*, September 26, 2013, http://mwnation.com/unfpa-rolls-out-a-national -condomise-campaign/.

60 percent of the condoms donated by various Western nations and organizations through UNFPA. How disturbing to see that while African youth are not being educated about the behaviors that are most conducive to their health and well-being, they are being "condomized".

From 1996 to 2000, Africa received an average of about 414 million donated condoms, but this number has increased exponentially to almost 2 billion condoms every year. This works out to almost $70 million spent on condoms.[22] In Africa this is an enormous amount of money; such an expense is outrageous to the ordinary men and women in Africa who are struggling to pay for food, water, medicine, transportation, and shelter. But for its architects and proponents, the CONDOMIZE! project is a top priority and serious business. Money is spent on unruly raves, parties, and bonfires to entice young people to accept free condoms. These events are seen as necessary health interventions, and African ministries of health, smaller government-run organizations, and nongovernmental organizations have fallen in line with the program so that they can benefit from the large funding stream.[23]

The Supremacy of Toxic Recommendations

Another popular but dubious strategy for fighting HIV infections is decriminalizing prostitution. At the 2014 International AIDS Conference in Melbourne Australia, Western experts claimed that decriminalizing "sex work"

---

[22] Ahmed et al., *Contraceptives and Condoms*.

[23] Lisa Shirichena, "Govt, UN agency unveil teen condoms", *Herald*, November 26, 2015, http://www.herald.co.zw/govt-un-agency-unveil-teen-condoms/.

would reduce HIV infections by 33 to 46 percent over the next decade.[24] They argued that because prostitution is illegal, sex workers do not have the same access to condoms and reproductive health care as other people do. Thus, HIV spreads more rapidly and is less likely to be detected and treated among sex workers and their clients. Bringing sex workers out of the shadows, they say, would allow them to adopt healthier behaviors.

But the people calling for decriminalization are ignoring the fact that it would keep millions of girls and women trapped, many against their will, in the sex industry, with little or no recourse for the outrages committed against them. Given the unspeakable abuse that women and girls endure in the sex industry, given the level of drug abuse to keep them silent and compliant, it is disconcerting that anyone would try to legitimize prostitution in the name of public health.

While experts are calling for prostitution to be destigmatized in order to fight HIV, they are also calling for HIV itself to be destigmatized. An example is the IPPF's publication *Healthy, Happy and Hot*.[25] The authors of the booklet describe it as a guide for the following:

- Young people who are living with HIV or who have a partner who is living with HIV
- Young people who have recently been diagnosed with HIV as well as those who have been living with HIV for a while or since birth

[24] Sarah Boseley, "Decriminalise Sex Work to Help Control AIDS Pandemic, Scientists Demand", *Guardian*, July 21, 2014, https://www.theguardian.com /society/2014/jul/22/decriminalise-sex-work-control-aids-scientists-demand.

[25] International Planned Parenthood Federation, *Healthy, Happy and Hot: A Young Person's Guide to Their Rights, Sexuality and Living with HIV* (n.p.: IPPF, 2010), p. 2, http://www.ippf.org/sites/default/files/healthy_happy_hot.pdf.

- Young people living with HIV who are married, in a relationship with one or more partners, as well as those who are single, dating, or just want to have sex
- Young people living with HIV who are just starting to think about dating and sex as well as those who have more experience
- Young people living with HIV: men, women, transgender people and those who are figuring out their gender identity
- Young people living with HIV who are interested in dating and having sex with people of the same sex or opposite sex, as well as those who are exploring and questioning their sexual orientation

So how does Planned Parenthood encourage young people with HIV to behave? Well, first they stress that "being in a relationship with someone who has HIV is just as fulfilling and satisfying as with anyone else."[26] One might not be able to compare his relationships, however, because the party with HIV is not obligated to disclose that he is infected with the virus: "Some countries have laws that say people living with HIV must tell their sexual partner(s) about their status before having sex, even if they use condoms or only engage in sexual activity with a low risk of giving HIV to someone else. These laws violate the rights of people living with HIV by forcing them to disclose or face the possibility of criminal charges."[27]

The booklet goes on to encourage HIV-positive people to enjoy sex in whatever way they want, regardless of the consequences to anyone else: "There is no right or wrong way to have sex. Just have fun, explore and be yourself!"[28]

[26] Ibid., p. 4.
[27] Ibid., p. 6
[28] Ibid., p. 7.

THE HYPERSEXUALIZATION OF YOUTH

It also encourages high-risk behavior: "Some people have sex when they have been drinking alcohol or using drugs. This is your choice.... If you want to have sex and think you might get drunk or high, plan ahead by bringing condoms and lube or putting them close to where you usually have sex."[29]

There are many other similar materials in circulation, and, in certain supposedly respectable quarters, these are considered "educative" and "evidence-based". Any attempt to criticize them is met with scorn. Thus the hypersexualization of African youth continues.

[29] Ibid., p. 11.

3

The Seeds of Radical Feminism

The Beauty and the Resilience
of the African Woman

African nations have their share of difficulties, limitations, and inadequacies. I grew up keenly aware of the imperfections of my society. Our hardships did not drown our decency, however, and we did not lose our humanity or devolve into barbarism. Instead, love, respect, service, decorum, modesty, and manners remained our ideals. Our high standards were mostly attributable to our women, for women tend to be the civilizing influence in a society.

My understanding of what it means to be a woman was impressed upon me by the many women I knew in my childhood—my grandmother, my mother, my friends' mothers, my mother's friends, my aunties, my sisters, my friends' sisters, my sisters' friends, my teachers, and many others. These women of different ages and socioeconomic situations projected grace, beauty, strength, and indomitable courage—all of which belong at the core of authentic femininity. Even in the face of pain and loss, they were resilient and faithful. They were, to me, the true picture of female excellence. They were real women of substance.

It was from these women, and not from Western ideologues, that I learned what it means to be an empowered and liberated woman. The women I admire use their freedom and their strength to practice their faith and to love their husbands and their children (born and unborn). According to the Western model of womanhood being imposed upon Africa, however, freedom is being "sexually liberated" and strength is being selfish, individualistic, and fiercely autonomous. Thankfully this model is not the bold, brilliant, beautiful brand of femininity I see in African women from Freetown, Sierra Leone, to Cape Town, South Africa. The African woman in her element contradicts the modern world, which tells her that faith means nothing, that marriage is whatever anyone wants it to be, that motherhood should be a unilateral choice, and that babies should be born only at the most convenient of times.

Elevating African Women, the Need for Authentic Feminism

It would be naïve of me to describe the African woman in glowing terms without also pointing out that in many African communities and cultures, the status and the situation of women is still a cause for concern and in need of much attention, work, and improvement. The persistence of cultural practices such as female genital mutilation (FGM) and child marriage have harmed millions of women and girls in many regions of the continent. A number of medical conditions continue to plague women and put them in very vulnerable positions in their communities; one of these is vesicovaginal fistula, which can result from being raped or from giving birth at a young age. And women still do not enjoy the same full rights and privileges as men in certain communities, such as those where women still cannot inherit and own lands or property.

It is important to understand that the situation of women in Africa varies greatly from one place to another. In those places where women are hindered in their development, there is need for a more emphatic and determined response to the mistreatment that crushes girls and women. African nations should unanimously decide to outlaw FGM and child marriage. There is real need to find and care for women and girls caught in the web of harmful practices in their communities. There should be a careful restructuring of those systems that allow women to fall through the cracks. Women should be given the opportunity to receive an education and to rise to their full stature, because when they rise, they lift their families and, by extension, their communities. This agenda is what authentic feminism should be about. It should seek to empower women so that they can develop their human potential and fully contribute to society. It should elevate downtrodden women so that they can radiate their goodness.

But instead of authentic feminism, a selfish and radical strain of feminism has risen in the West and has gained an international platform and a place of prominence in this century.

Radical Feminism and the Weaponization of Womanhood in the West

In its early days, the feminist movement was about advocating for the recognition and the protection of women in society. It focused on obtaining for women the basic legal rights to pursue an education, choose a profession, own or inherit property, manage a business, and share custody of children in the case of divorce. The most prominent feminist issue was women's suffrage, the right to vote.

First-wave feminists struggled for the recognition of women as equal to men in dignity and worth, while still retaining protections for them as wives and mothers. This first step was a necessary and worthy cause, and it was attained and fulfilled in most of the Western world by the middle of the twentieth century.

The early 1960s saw the rise of second-wave feminism, which insisted on moving women away from the core aspects of femininity, namely, those attributes necessary for motherhood—fertility, receptivity, and generosity. Whereas first-wave feminism was mostly about property rights and voting rights, second-wave feminism was about defining and asserting the reproductive rights of women, which included the right to sexual pleasure outside of marriage, contraception, no-fault divorce, and ultimately, abortion.

The Soviet Union was the first formerly Christian country to legalize abortion on demand for the purpose of sexual revolution. After the idea of sexual revolution migrated to North America and Europe, in the United Kingdom, the United States, and Canada, restrictions on abortion were removed through either powerful legislative maneuvers or heavy-handed judicial rulings. New language was developed by feminist activists to rationalize the killing of the unborn. New phrases such as "blob of tissue", "right to choose", "reproductive justice", "right to privacy", and "bodily autonomy" were created to gloss over the reality that abortion kills an innocent human being.

By the 1990s third-wave feminism set in, and its advocates started challenging binaries (such as male and female, father and mother) as artificial social constructs. The core of this brand of feminism is the celebration of self-determined sexuality as a means of female empowerment. As a result, third-wave feminism promotes personal, individualized views on gender-related issues, such as prostitution, pornography, sadomasochism, and transgenderism.

Many third-wave feminists support the notion that commercial sex work is a legitimate form of employment and oppose the view that women who participate in pornography and prostitution are exploited.[1]

Third-wave feminism has become mainstream, and like all modern sexual-liberationist ideologies, it is being propagated throughout the world. It is being mimicked and echoed by African feminist groups as they embrace queer theory, abortion rights, LGBT propaganda, and commercial sex work, all of which are considered foreign and even opposed to most African cultures.

Bowing and Bending before the Throne of Western Feminism

In 2006 one hundred African feminists gathered for the first African Feminist Forum in Accra, Ghana, where they drafted and adopted a new charter of feminist principles. According to their joint statement, the purpose of their gathering was "to chart ways to strengthen and grow the feminist movement on the continent".[2] The *Charter of Feminist Principles for African Feminists* is a sixteen-page document that reads like a statement from any Western second- or third-wave feminist group.

The charter announces the firm commitment to "dismantle patriarchy" in all its manifestations in Africa.[3] Yet

---

[1] J.A. Fisher, "Today's Feminism: A Brief Look at Third-Wave Feminism", *Being Feminist* (blog), May 16, 2013, excerpts from paragraphs 6 and 8, https://beingfeministblog.wordpress.com/2013/05/16/todays-feminism-a-brief-look-at-third-wave-feminism/.

[2] African Feminist Forum, *Charter of Feminist Principles for African Feminists* (Accra, Ghana: AFF, 2006), p. 1, http://awdf.org/wp-content/uploads/Charter_of_Feminist_Principles_for_African_Feminists.pdf.

[3] Ibid., p. 2.

the document does not mention the horrors, such as FGM and child marriage, done to women in certain parts of Africa. Instead, it faithfully regurgitates the shallow first-world problems often touted by Western modern-day feminists. It calls for "freedom of choice and autonomy regarding bodily integrity issues, including reproductive rights, abortion, sexual identity and sexual orientation".[4]

The charter conspicuously fails to recognize the irreplaceable role of African women as mothers, wives, educators, homemakers, nurses, and caregivers who, through their generous, receptive, and maternal nature, humanize, civilize, nurture, and transform their communities. In fact, the words "mother", "wife", and "family" are not mentioned in the document. Instead, the document is filled with antagonism toward men and traditional female roles; it opposes "the subversion and/or hijacking of autonomous feminist spaces to serve right wing, conservative agendas".[5] So, from their guiding principles, modern-day African feminists have firmly bound themselves to left-wing politics and, by so doing, have declared their allegiance to the Western feminist agenda. Meanwhile the document claims that "it is a profound insult to claim that feminism was imported into Africa from the west."[6]

A growing number of feminist groups across the continent of Africa follow the principles mapped out by this charter and other similarly worded documents. They all pride themselves on being original, but in reality they bear the stamp of second- and third-wave Western feminism by supporting abortion extremism and distorted views of human sexuality while rejecting the traditional roles of wife

[4] Ibid., p. 11.
[5] Ibid., p. 14.
[6] Ibid., p. 8.

and mother, which are highly esteemed in Africa. As the willing collaborators of Western feminist activists who are desperately seeking the globalization of their radical agenda, they are denying and betraying their own people. These new African feminists contrast sharply with their forebears, who labored for women's recognition, well-being, and empowerment in Africa.

One of the great early African feminists was the late Wangari Maathai, the renowned environmental and political activist who, in 2004, became the first African woman to receive a Nobel Peace Prize for her contribution to sustainable development, democracy, and peace. In a conversation with Norway's *Dagen* newspaper, Maathai spoke quite clearly about abortion: "Abortion is wrong. There is no reason why someone who is conceived will not be given the opportunity to be born and to live a happy life."[7] She also criticized the West "for influencing other countries to introduce abortion. We know that many countries do not want to join that view and practice, for they perceive abortion as killing unborn children." About abortion in her home country of Kenya, Maathai said, "It is impossible to introduce abortion, and it is unlikely or reasonable that abortion will be supported and approved by the government. This is a mainly Christian country, a very Christian country, and it will be considered immoral and unacceptable." So Maathai was against not only abortion but also the extreme interventionism and imperialistic interference of the West on the issue.

The mind-set of this fearless African feminist is consistent with the cultural and legal framework of her people.

[7] "Nobelprisvinneren er kristen abortmotstander", *Dagen*, December 8, 2004, http://www.dagen.no/Innenriks/Nobelprisvinneren_er_kristen_abort motstander-32112.

Hers is the kind of feminism that will not bend before the throne of Western feminism. Maathai's sort of feminism can help African women to thrive and flourish. It is the brand of feminism that is needed in every part of Africa.

Understanding the Umbilical Cord

Women's organizations—based on religious, tribal, geographic, professional, or trade-union interests—have proliferated across Africa and are networking throughout the continent on an unprecedented scale. The Catholic Women's Association, the Network of African Rural Women's Association, the Federation of Business and Professional Women, the Christian Mother's Guild, the Federation of Muslim Women's Association, Women in Aviation, the Association of University Women—there are indeed hundreds, if not thousands, of such groups in every African country, but they are not to be conflated with the feminist movement, particularly its Westernized version, which is a more recent phenomenon in Africa.

Whereas most African women's organizations highly regard their members' mothering and caregiving roles, the emerging feminist groups in Africa think little of these. The core of their cause is to champion a particular interpretation of reproductive health and rights. They also are very noticeably anti-male. The largest and most prominent of the new feminist groups are intricately connected to major Western stakeholders who support them with funding and training. By this means, Western third-wave feminist organizations are spreading in Africa.

One of these organizations is the African Women's Development Fund (AWDF), which hosts the biennial African Feminist Forum, at which the *Charter of Feminist Principles for African Feminists* was adopted. The AWDF is committed to spreading the feminist agenda in Africa through funding local projects that align with their work, and for this they receive more than $4 million every year, most of which is provided by major Western donors. These include:

Gates Foundation
Open Society Foundations
Ford Foundation
Global Fund for Women
Mama Cash
Match International Women's Fund, Canada
Women's Foundation of Minnesota
Women's Funding Network, U.S.A
Department for International Development
Norwegian Agency for Development Cooperation
United Nations Women
Dutch MDG3[8]

Another major African feminist organization with significant links to Western organizations is the African Women's Development and Communication Network (FEMNET). It is perhaps the most active campaigner in Africa for abortion rights. Its major partners and supporters include:

Ford Foundation
Global Fund for Women
Oxfam Novib
Urgent Action Fund–Africa

[8] "Donors", African Women's Development Fund, http://awdf.org/donors/; Jessica Horn, "African Feminists Mark Women's Role in Shaping Their Continent's Future", Open Society Foundations, May 12, 2016, https://www.opensocietyfoundations.org/voices/african-feminists-mark-women-s-role-shaping-their-continent-s-future.

International Women's Health Coalition
Ipas Africa Alliance
Swedish Association for Sexuality Education
Equality Now
Fredskorpset
Hivos
International Planned Parenthood Federation
Family Care International
Embassy of Sweden
African Women's Development Fund[9]

Again, an overwhelming majority of these donors are Western organizations and governments. At least two of them (Ipas and IPPF) are active international abortion promoters and providers. A number of them are involved in developing and promoting comprehensive sexuality education, which targets and hypersexualizes children.

Another feminist force in Africa is the Solidarity for African Women's Rights (SOAWR), a coalition of organizations that lobby and push for the ratification and domestication of the Protocol to the African Charter on Human and Peoples' Rights on the Rights of Women in Africa, also known as the Maputo Protocol. This treaty, adopted in 2003 by most nations of the African Union, has been rightly recognized by many as a backdoor means of introducing legal abortion in all the fifty-four countries of the African Union. SOAWR was formed to campaign, mobilize, and lobby at both national and regional levels for the Protocol. And so far, they have made many inroads in many countries because of the generous donations made by the same Westerners who are keen to trigger the kinds of social change that will eclipse African values on the

---

[9] FEMNET, *2014 Annual Report*, November 8, 2015, p. 8, http://femnet .co/wp-content/uploads/2015/11/FEMNET-2014-Annual-Report-.pdf.

sanctity of life and the dignity of sexuality. Here are some of the major SOAWR donors:

Ford Foundation
Global Fund for Women
Open Society Foundations
Embassy of Sweden
Hivos
Mama Cash
African Women's Development Fund
Oxfam GB
Oxfam Novib
Sigrid Rausing Trust
Action Aid International[10]

This list is eerily similar to the AWDF's and FEMNET's donor lists. There is much inbreeding in the new feminist movement in Africa as Western donors fall over each other to fund new efforts in fresh territory. Organizations such as FEMNET, the AWDF, and SOAWR are the new African wineskins being filled to the brim with the intoxicating ideology of their benefactors. The new colonial masters are using donations to recreate Africa in their own image, through the introduction of their ideas about sex, freedom, and human development.

Maputo Protocol, the Map to Legal Abortion in Africa

The Maputo Protocol was supposed to be a major step to ensure the advancement and empowerment of African

[10] "SOAWR's Funders", SOAWR, http://www.soawr.org/content/soawr's -funders.

women through the protection of various rights. Its twenty-
five articles address various issues or rights:

Article 1: Definitions
Article 2: Elimination of Discrimination against Women
Article 3: Right to Dignity
Article 4: The Rights to Life, Integrity and Security of
the Person
Article 5: Elimination of Harmful Practices (referring
to female genital mutilation and other harmful tradi-
tional practices)
Article 6: Marriage
Article 7: Separation, Divorce and Annulment of
Marriage
Article 8: Access to Justice and Equal Protection before
the Law
Article 9: Right to Participation in the Political and
Decision-Making Process
Article 10: Right to Peace
Article 11: Protection of Women in Armed Conflicts
Article 12: Right to Education and Training
Article 13: Economic and Social Welfare Rights
Article 14: Health and Reproductive Rights
Article 15: Right to Food Security
Article 16: Right to Adequate Housing
Article 17: Right to Positive Cultural Context
Article 18: Right to a Healthy and Sustainable
Environment
Article 19: Right to Sustainable Development
Article 20: Widows' Rights
Article 21: Right to Inheritance
Article 22: Special Protection of Elderly Women
Article 23: Special Protection of Women with Disabilities
Article 24: Special Protection of Women in Distress
Article 25: Remedies

These are inarguably some of the most basic rights that women (as well as men) should enjoy in every free and civilized society, but controversy crept in with the interpretation of and the full definition given to a few of these rights, especially the right elucidated in article 14: health and reproductive rights.

Of course, the reproductive health of African women should be a key issue for this body of African nations. With unacceptably high rates of maternal mortality, child marriage, sexual exploitation, violence against women, sexually transmitted diseases such as HIV/AIDS, and the trafficking of African women in sex slavery, the subject matter of article 14 is not only good but most necessary in a protocol such as this. In the last paragraph of this brief article, however, abortion rights were inserted. The article enjoined the signatories to take all appropriate measures to "protect the reproductive rights of women by authorising medical abortion in cases of sexual assault, rape, incest, and where the continued pregnancy endangers the mental and physical health of the mother or the life of the mother or the foetus." These forty words became the blueprint for legalizing abortion in all the member states of the African Union.

One of the organizations that helped to draft and subsequently lobbied for this provision was Equality Now, founded in New York in 1992. The African regional office of this organization, in collaboration with the Ethiopian Women Lawyers Association and FEMNET, convened like-minded African women's organizations in January 2003. According to a synopsis by Mary Wandia, one of the cofounding members of SOAWR who also works with Equality Now:

> The meeting pooled proposals and integrated them into a Draft Protocol highlighting weak provisions and proposing

language in a collective mark-up to align it with international standards. A multi-pronged advocacy strategy for the adoption of the proposals by the AU Secretariat and member states was also developed. After the meeting, the organisations met AU Secretariat officials and successfully advocated for the experts and ministerial meetings on the Protocol to be scheduled for March 2003.

Thereafter, the organisations embarked on national level advocacy targeting ministries of Justice and Gender to: adopt the proposals to strengthen the draft, confirm their participation in the AU experts and ministerial meetings, commit to send delegates with legal and human rights expertise from their capitals and to include women's rights organisations in the official delegations.

Prior to the Experts and Ministerial Meetings Equality Now's Africa Regional Office convened a second meeting of women's rights activists and organisations and an informal meeting with Permanent Representatives to the African Union, in order to ensure that the substantive provisions of the draft Protocol were strengthened during the experts and ministerial meetings.[11]

The resulting draft protocol "not only met but superseded international human rights standards on women's rights". The high-level advocacy and aggressive lobbying reek of massive funding and ideological manipulation. And they yielded results when the draft was subsequently adopted on July 11, 2003, by the African Union Assembly of Heads of State and Government; fifty-one of the fifty-four member states had signed the protocol as of 2017. Thirty-six signatories have ratified it; fifteen of the countries that signed

[11] "Tracing the Birth of and Advocacy for the Ratification and Implementation of the AU Protocol on Women's Rights—Mary Wandia", SOAWR, http://www.soawr.org/blog/tracing-birth-and-advocacy-ratification-and-implementation-au-protocol-women's-rights-mary.

it have not yet ratified it, and three countries (Tunisia, Egypt, and Botswana) have still not signed or ratified the Maputo Protocol.

Some African countries resisted by registering their reservations to some of the protocol's articles. Burundi, Senegal, Sudan, Rwanda, and Libya had reservations with article 14. Tunisia, Sudan, Kenya, Namibia, and South Africa recorded reservations about some of the marriage clauses. Egypt, Libya, Sudan, South Africa, and Zambia had reservations about "judicial separation, divorce and annulment of marriage".

In spite of these reservations, the Maputo Protocol has remained a treaty instrument of the African Union that is binding on all the countries that ratify it. For this reason, well-funded feminist organizations have continued to campaign for the ratification of the protocol by the various countries that adopted it.

SOAWR is a coalition organization formed for this purpose. And they described one of their main strategies as joint fund-raising to enable member organizations of SOAWR to carry out campaigns for ratification at the national level. In their own words: "Oxfam GB successfully raised funds to support SOAWR campaigns (under the Raising Her Voice Project) for ratification and/or implementation of the Protocol in seven countries; The Gambia, Liberia, Mozambique, Nigeria, South Africa, Tanzania and Uganda."[12] Again, the unseen manipulative hands of the neocolonial masters continue to be felt throughout Africa.

With regard to the part of the protocol that deals specifically with abortion, it has not had much of an impact on abortion law except in a few countries. Abortion

[12] Ibid.

remains mostly illegal in most African countries. In recent years, however, much effort has been made to shame and to move member states of the African Union that have signed or ratified the Maputo Protocol to remove their legal restrictions on abortion. One of the determined efforts was a strong recommendation and persistent call for the domestication of article 14 of the Maputo Protocol during the ordinary session of the African Union held in Luanda, Angola, in April 2014. The African Commission on Human and People's Rights issued an exhaustive document, titled *General Comment 2 on Article 14.1 (a), (b), (c) and (f) and Article 14.2 (a) and (c) of the Protocol to the African Charter on Human and Peoples' Rights on the Rights of Women in Africa*, which interprets the terms of that article. This document surprisingly takes a strong pro-abortion position. From its preface onward it is replete with the dubious language of "choice" and social change. What is more remarkable is how out of touch it is with the voice of ordinary Africans. Its preface was written and signed by Commissioner Soyata Maiga, special rapporteur on the rights of women in Africa. She stated:

> It should be noted that the Maputo Protocol is the very first treaty to recognize abortion, under certain conditions, as women's human right which they should enjoy without restriction or fear of being prosecuted.
>
> The African Commission on Human and Peoples' Rights (the African Commission) welcomes the ratification of this important instrument by the majority of AU Member States. However, the African Commission notes that many countries are yet to undertake the necessary legislative reforms towards domesticating the relevant provisions, including in the area of women's sexual and reproductive rights. As such, in many States Parties, there

is still limited access by women and girls to family planning, criminalization of abortion, and difficulties faced by women in accessing safe and available abortion services, including in cases where abortion is legalized.[13]

Maiga mentioned the strong pro-abortion entity whose voice is echoed throughout the *General Comment 2 on Article 14*: "The African Commission wishes to express its gratitude to Ipas Africa Alliance for its valuable contribution on all issues relating to sexual and reproductive rights and its technical support towards the preparation of the General Comment."[14]

Ipas Africa Alliance was established in 2000 by Ipas, an American abortion-promoting nongovernmental organization (NGO) whose mission is to increase the availability of "high-quality comprehensive abortion care; and to advocate for policies that advance women's reproductive health and rights across the continent".[15] So the African Commission had Ipas, a pro-abortion organization, serve as technical support for the drafting of this general comment, even though the majority of African people are repulsed by the practice of abortion. Ipas seemed very pleased with the result. Naisola Likimani, a senior policy adviser, stated: "For advocates and governments alike, General Comment 2 serves as a blueprint for action to save women's lives and

[13] Soyata Maiga, preface to *General Comment No. 2 on Article 14.1 (a), (b), (c) and (f) and Article 14.2 (a) and (c) of the Protocol to the African Charter on Human and Peoples' Rights on the Rights of Women in Africa*, by African Commission on Human and Peoples' Rights (Banjul, the Gambia: African Commission on Human and Peoples' Rights, 2014), p. 2, http://www.achpr.org/files/instruments/general-comments-rights-women/achpr_instr_general_comment2_rights_of_women_in_africa_eng.pdf.

[14] Ibid., p. 3.

[15] "Africa Alliance", Ipas, http://www.ipas.org/en/Where-We-Work/Africa/Africa-Alliance.aspx?m=1.

ensure they can realize their right to reproductive health across Africa and beyond."[16]

It is indeed a blueprint and comprehensive guide to introducing legal abortion throughout Africa. It disparages the cultural and religious beliefs of the African people with regard to their views on sex and the sanctity of human life from conception, which the document refers to as "barriers":

> The right to health care without discrimination requires State parties to remove impediments to the health services reserved for women, including ideology or belief-based barriers. Administrative laws, policies and procedures of health systems and structures cannot restrict access to family planning/contraception on the basis of religious beliefs.[17]

The African Commission expects governments to remove laws against abortion in section 46:

> State parties should provide a legal and social environment that is conducive to the exercise by women of their sexual and reproductive rights. This involves revisiting, if necessary, restrictive laws, policies and administrative procedures relating to family planning/contraception and safe abortion in the cases provided for in the Protocol, as well as integrating the provisions of the said legal instrument into domestic law.[18]

They also target youth by recommending that they be educated about "sexual and reproductive rights issues".

---

[16] "New Guidance for Upholding Reproductive Rights in Africa", Ipas, February 12, 2015, http://www.ipas.org/en/News/2015/February/New -guidance-for-upholding-reproductive-rights-in-Africa.aspx?m=1.

[17] African Commission on Human and Peoples' Rights, *General Comment No. 2*, p. 9.

[18] Ibid., p. 13.

The recommendation applies even to students in faith-based schools:

> In addition, State parties must ensure that educational institutions at primary, secondary and tertiary levels include sexual and reproductive rights issues in their school programs and to take the necessary measures so those programs also reach women in private schools, including faith-based schools, as well as those out of school.[19]

In section 58, the African Commission targets healthcare workers and even recommends that midwives and other healthcare workers be trained to become abortionists:

> State parties should avoid all unnecessary or irrelevant restrictions on the profile of the service providers authorized to practice safe abortion and the requirements of multiple signatures or approval of committees, in the cases provided for in the Protocol. In many African countries, there are not enough trained physicians available. Mid-level providers such as midwives and other health workers should be trained to provide safe abortion care.[20]

With these radical interpretations and expectations, it is obvious that article 14 was incorporated into the Maputo Protocol in order to open the door to legal abortion throughout the continent. Although it is not the longest or most detailed of the articles in the original Maputo Protocal, article 14 has become the one most lobbied, campaigned, and promoted by Western-funded feminist organizations across Africa. Millions of dollars have been given to weaponize the forty words of the article that provide a license to kill Africa's unborn children.

[19] Ibid., p. 14.
[20] Ibid., p. 15

4

The Push for Abortion Rights

Vox Populi—The Sanctity of Human Life in Africa

I have a brother whose middle name is Ndubisi, which in Igbo means "Life is paramount", "Life is the beginning", or "Life is first." I never gave much thought to the full meaning of this name until recently, when I was reflecting on the views of my people regarding the sanctity of human life. I realized that one can tell a lot about a people's beliefs from the names they give their children. Naming a child is an opportunity for parents to tell the world around them what is most important to them. Here are some other common names in my native language.

Chinwendu	God owns life
Chijindu	God sustains life
Ndubueze	Life is supreme
Ndudi	There is life

These were the names I heard growing up, the names of my friends, classmates, and playmates. We were the little bearers of our parents' deepest thoughts and prayers. To my mind, the culture of life that gave rise to these names cannot coexist with a culture of death that aborts its unwanted children.

At the core of my people's value system is the profound recognition that human life is precious, paramount, and supreme. For us, abortion, which is the deliberate killing of little ones in the womb, is a direct attack on innocent human life. It is a serious injustice, which no one should have the right to commit.

This view of abortion is shared by people in many other parts of Africa, beyond my own tribe and city. I have traveled throughout the continent, and the over-whelming majority of the people I have met—people of all ages, backgrounds, professions, socioeconomic classes, and religious affiliations—have expressed the same firm respect for the inestimable value of every human life from conception to natural death. Lest my experiences be dismissed as purely anecdotal, surveys corroborate my findings. A 2014 study by Ipsos, for example found that 87 percent of Kenyans oppose abortion on demand.[1] This nationwide survey echoed the findings of a 2013 global study by Pew Research Center that asked 40,117 respondents in forty countries what they thought about various moral issues, including abortion. The vast major-ity of Africans said that abortion was morally unaccept-able: 92 percent of Ghanaians, 88 percent of Ugandans, 82 percent of Kenyans, 80 percent of Nigerians, and 77 percent of Tunisians said that they considered abortion to be morally wrong.

The number of Africans opposed to abortion contrasts starkly with the number of abortion opponents in first-world countries. In the same Pew study, 14 percent of the

---

[1] Pew Research Center, "Global Views on Morality" (2013 poll), http://www.pewglobal.org/2014/04/15/global-morality/.

French who were surveyed, 19 percent of the Germans, 25 percent of the British, and 26 percent of the Canadians disapproved of abortion.[2] Perhaps Africans tend to oppose abortion because safely bringing healthy babies into the world is more difficult in Africa than in developing countries. Perhaps Africans are more grateful for every pregnancy and every successful delivery, and, for that matter, for every dawn they rise to see, because they have a deeper awareness of the precariousness of life.

The Legal Abortion Landscape in Africa

Nevertheless, the push to legalize abortion is gaining ground in Africa. Laws vary greatly from one country to the next. I have grouped below the fifty-four African countries into four categories that reflect these differences.

In the following twenty-two countries abortion is prohibited or allowed only to save the life of the mother:

Angola

Central African Republic

Congo-Brazzaville

Democratic Republic
   of the Congo

Côte d'Ivoire

Djibouti

Gabon

The Gambia

Guinea-Bissau

Lesotho

Libya

Madagascar

Malawi

Mauritania

Nigeria

São Tomé and Príncipe

Senegal

Sierra Leone

Somalia

South Sudan

Tanzania

Uganda

[2] Ibid.

Abortion is legally permitted for one of several reasons (subject to medical, psychological, or legal review) in twenty-five countries. Reasons could be physical health, mental health, rape, incest, or defects in the fetus.

Algeria	Liberia
Benin	Mali
Botswana	Mauritius
Burkina Faso	Morocco
Burundi	Namibia
Cameroon	Niger
Chad	Rwanda
Comoros	Seychelles
Egypt	Sudan
Equatorial Guinea	Swaziland
Ghana	Togo
Guinea	Zimbabwe
Kenya	

Abortion is permitted for the reasons given for the previous category and also for economic and social reasons in these three countries:

Eritrea	Zambia
Ethiopia	

Abortion on demand is legal in four countries.

Cape Verde	South Africa
Mozambique	Tunisia[3]

[3] Global Life Campaign, "196 Nations Grouped by Life-Protecting or Abortion Policies", *Abortion Worldwide Report*, January 20, 2017, https://docs.wixstatic.com/ugd/cacd2b_bcae7a2748d9483a8f1b53288d4e4538.pdf.

Almost 80 percent of African countries have some sort of law prohibiting or restricting abortion, and it is predicated on the widely held belief that unborn babies have a right to life and deserve to be protected by law. With this prevalent view on the issue of abortion, most people are satisfied with these laws. And as of 2017, there are hardly any locally organized complaints, demonstrations, or protests calling for the legalization of abortion. On the contrary, there have been many pro-life rallies, marches, and conferences in various countries, expressing the people's desire for the continued protection of the unborn.

Even in those countries where abortion on demand is legal, the majority of the people still hold fast to their belief that human life in the womb is sacred and that abortion is morally unacceptable. For example, a Pew survey showed that 77 percent of Tunisians and 61 percent of South Africans found abortion unacceptable even though abortion on demand is legal in their countries.[4]

If the majority of Africans are against abortion, who is pushing for the legalization of abortion in Africa? In 2014, the abortion-promoting organization Ipas published *Human Rights and African Abortion Laws*, a handbook for judges that targets African restrictions on abortion. The handbook portrays these restrictions as "barriers" to accessing abortion services that must be removed. These so-called barriers include authorization and performance of the procedure by a doctor, parental notification or consent for an abortion performed on a minor, and limits on the gestational age of the child to be aborted.[5] In other words,

---

[4] Pew Research Center, "Global Views on Morality".

[5] Prof. Charles Ngwena, *Human Rights and African Abortion Laws: A Handbook for Judges* (Nairobi: Ipas Africa Alliance, 2014), p. 34, http://www.kelinkenya .org/wp-content/uploads/2015/12/HANDBOOK-ON-AFRICAN -ABORTION-LAWS.pdf.

Ipas is pushing abortion on demand throughout Africa. And the organization also demands that healthcare professionals who are morally opposed to abortion be forced by their governments to refer women seeking abortions to those willing to perform them.

Ipas is not the only organization that is pushing abortion in Africa. Its list of barriers to abortion was taken mostly from the 2012 World Health Organization (WHO) publication *Safe Abortion: Technical and Policy Guidance for Health Systems.*[6] All the international pro-abortion organizations hinge their agenda on the WHO, which has taken an unambiguous position in support of worldwide abortion on demand. Its publication on "safe abortion" presents the public-health and human rights arguments for abortion, the various methods of abortion, the planning and the managing of abortion services, and the financing of abortion facilities. It does not, however, explain anything pertaining to the gestational development of the unborn child whose life is to be terminated. It never once uses the word "baby" or "child". Nor does it indicate the possibility of psychological pain or physical difficulties following an abortion.

Misplaced Priorities

In their attempts to legalize abortion across Africa, abortion advocates say that legalized abortion is a way to reduce high maternal mortality rates. This claim has become a dangling carrot before a starving donkey, because African countries

---

[6] World Health Organization, *Safe Abortion: Technical and Policy Guidance for Health Systems*, 2nd ed. (Geneva: World Health Organization, 2012), www .who.int/iris/bitstream/10665/70914/1/9789241548434_eng.pdf, p. 94.

want, by all means, to reduce their shamefully high maternal mortality rates. Consequently, African leaders are vulnerable to the argument that the killing of unborn babies should be legalized and even supported by their governments to reduce deaths of pregnant women. This apparent solution, however, will not solve the problem in question.

Apart from the moral question of whether an abortion is ever justified to save the life of a woman, it is important to determine the causes of maternal deaths and whether abortions could prevent them. According to a WHO systematic analysis of global causes of maternal deaths, hemorrhage (bleeding) accounts for 27.1 percent of them, hypertensive disorders 14 percent, sepsis 10.7 percent, and embolism 3.2 percent. Other direct causes of death (such as obstructed labor) account for 9.6 percent. Less than 8 percent of maternal deaths are linked to abortion, and it is important to note that some of these occur in regions of the world that have had legal abortion for decades.[7]

Since hemorrhage, hypertension, and sepsis are responsible for more than half of the maternal deaths worldwide, efforts to save lives should be directed toward fortifying healthcare systems in areas such as blood-transfusion services, sepsis treatment, and hypertension management. Yet at international forums and events that purport to be concerned with maternal health, "safe abortion" is cited many more times than all of these life-saving methods combined. In fact, the legalization of abortion, increased abortion accessibility, and increased contraception prevalence for women seem to be the main policy strategies put forward at most of these events.

---

[7] Lale Say et al., "Global Causes of Maternal Death: A WHO Systematic Analysis", *Lancet* 2, no. 6 (June 2014), http://dx.doi.org/10.1016/S2214 -109X(14)70227-X.

Sub-Saharan African nations are the most affected by this skewed attention on abortion, because postpartum bleeding is a real killer in those countries, which are still a long way from solving this problem. Studies show that in all the maternal deaths caused by bleeding, more than half of them occur in sub-Saharan Africa,[8] which has some of the most inadequate blood-transfusion services in the world—a fact that receives little mention, if any, in the fight against maternal deaths. Also not mentioned is that women who die from excessive bleeding cannot be saved by abortion when a hemorrhage begins after their babies are born.

The WHO estimates that a blood donation rate of 1 percent would meet a nation's most basic blood requirements. The median blood-donation rate is 3.68 percent in high-income countries, 1.17 percent in middle-income countries, and only 0.39 percent in low-income countries. All of the sub-Saharan African countries were below the 1 percent threshold of minimum required blood donations. Apart from South Africa and Botswana, most of these countries were below 0.5 percent.[9] This insufficient blood supply is the major reason hundreds of thousands of African women die in childbirth, yet this fact is hardly ever discussed meaningfully in public forums.

The tragedy of maternal death will not be solved by contraception and abortion, but by determining the causes

[8] Lale Say et al., "Subgroup Analysis of Haemorrhage Deaths by Millennium Development Goal Region", table 2 in "Global Causes of Maternal Death", http://www.thelancet.com/action/showFullTableImage?tableId=tbl2&pii=S2214109X1470227X.

[9] Tanja Z. Zanin et al., "Tapping into a Vital Resource: Understanding the Motivators and Barriers to Blood Donation in Sub-Saharan Africa", *African Journal of Emergency Medicine* 6, no. 2 (June 2016), http://dx.doi.org/10.1016/j.afjem.2016.02.003.

of maternal death and addressing them. There is no telling how many lives could be saved if even a fraction of the billions of dollars being spent by Western donors on contraception and abortion in Africa were directed toward improving the quality of obstetric care.

Abortion by Stealth: Imo, Nigeria

As we have seen, most Africans disapprove of abortion. Thus, the legalization and expansion of abortion in Africa is rarely made public or covered by the media. In other words, changes in abortion laws are made by stealth, without Africans being informed about them.

A case in point is the 2013 legalization of abortion in my home state, Imo, Nigeria. The original bill introduced in the state assembly was entitled "Imo State Law of Nigeria Violence against Persons (Prohibition) Law No. 12", and was passed and silently signed by Governor Rochas Okorocha in order to stop all forms of violence, including physical, physiological, and domestic. Like most bills, it was very long and rather dry. But unlike most bills, it was kept secret from the people, because buried in its hundreds of paragraphs and thousands of words, was the right to abortion. According to section 40:

> (h) Every woman shall have the rights to take decisions about her health needs and requirement. In particular, she shall have the right to determine the process concerning reproduction in her body.
> (i) Every woman shall have the right to enjoy reproductive rights including the right to medical abortion in cases of sexual assault, rape, incest and where the continued pregnancy endangers the life or the physical, mental, physiological or emotional health of the mother.

There it was, the bill within the bill: the abortion liber-alization law within the violence-prohibition law. How ironic that an anti-violence bill was used to usher in a horrific form of violence—the violent killing of unborn children. Abortion proponents always seem willing to go to any length and to use any opportunity to get what they want, which is the permission to kill the baby in the womb.

The support for this bill did not come from the peo-ple of Imo, but from the Women's Global Network for Reproductive Rights (WGNRR), a pro-abortion orga-nization founded in the Netherlands and funded by the Swedish International Development Agency, the Norwe-gian Agency for Development Cooperation, the Danish International Development Agency, the Danish Ministry of Foreign Affairs, the Ford Foundation, the MacArthur Foundation, the Global Fund for Women, Mama Cash, and many other wealthy Western donors. This well-funded Dutch organization, with a rather colonial attitude, had much to say about the Imo law in its "Solidarity State-ment to Celebrate the Imo Abortion Law":

> We congratulate the Nigeria SRHR movement for pushing for it and the Imo State House of Assembly with its successful enactment. This victory is an advance for women not only in Imo state, but in Nigeria as a whole, as it guarantees women's rights to enjoy the highest level of physical, mental and social well-being, health care ser-vices, including those related to full access to modern contraceptive methods, adequate health care facilities, information and counseling; they shall have the right to exercise their reproductive choice; and enjoy their reproductive rights including the right to safe and legal abortion.

The statement continues:

> Keeping this important victory in mind, WGNRR would
> like to echo his vigilance in the implementation of the
> law. We wish to remind the Imo State officials that any
> law without efficient implementation and accountability
> mechanisms remains a dead letter.

The WGNRR then encouraged other states in Nigeria and countries throughout Africa to review their laws
and policies for ways to advance sexual and reproductive
rights for women and girls, including access to safe and
legal abortion.[10] This meddling puts African people in a
position inferior to that of wealthy Westerners. It is a form
of cultural supremacy, even imperialism, which should
be unacceptable.

While the Western cultural imperialists celebrated the
Imo law, the people of Imo rightly recognized it as another
manifestation of the culture of death that is being injected
into their society. Women, men, and children of all ages
took to the streets in protest. Their demand was a simple
one: that the governor immediately repeal the sections of
the new law that legalize abortion. After a few days of pro-
life protests, life won over death, and the governor made
a public apology to the people of Imo for signing the bill.
While signing the repeal papers, Governor Okorocha
admitted that his decision was due to public outcry over the
law, especially from religious leaders and traditional rulers.[11]

---

[10] Women's Global Network for Reproductive Rights, "Nigeria: Solidarity Statement to Celebrate the Imo Abortion Law", http://www.september28
.org/nigeria-solidarity-statement-to-celebrate-the-imo-state-abortion-law/.

[11] "Imo Government Repeals Abortion Law", Channels Television, October
4, 2013, http://www.channelstv.com/2013/10/04/imo-government-repeals
-abortion-law/.

Abortion by Stealth: Freetown, Sierra Leone

The Imo bill was not the first or the last attempt to push Africans to legitimatize abortion. Sierra Leone was pressured into a similar position in December 2015, barely a year after surviving the Ebola crisis. Under intense lobbying efforts by the same well-known pro-abortion organizations, the parliament of Sierra Leone passed the Safe Abortion Bill of 2015. The bill, which had been in parliament for at least three years, had been proposed by Isatu Kabia. To persuade other lawmakers to vote for the bill, Kabia cited a United Nations committee that had examined Sierra Leone according to the 2014 Convention on the Elimination of All Forms of Discrimination against Women and found the country wanting. The committee took exception to

> the fact that the law on abortion criminalizes the procedure without providing any exception, the high incidence of sexual violence and unwanted pregnancies resulting in unsafe abortions, which account for 13 per cent of maternal mortality, and delays in adopting the abortion bill, which decriminalizes the termination of pregnancy based on various socioeconomic grounds.[12]

Needless to say, the committee recommended that Sierra Leone pass the pending abortion bill, and its voice of authority was the powerful wind that propelled Kabia's final appeal to parliament. No wonder the bill passed.

[12] Committee on the Elimination of Discrimination against Women, *Concluding Observations on the Sixth Periodic Report of Sierra Leone*, March 10, 2014, pp. 10–11, section 32(d), http://docstore.ohchr.org/SelfServices/FilesHandler .ashx?enc=6QkG1d%2FPPRiCAqhKb7yhskcAJS%2FU4wb%2BdIVicv Go5Rwy8s5lACxMFIDPe%2BCAsVaF617GRAk9d%2FSkb3zNovIsglv RIq31tFzdUWqKrdONourUWAt3IYt90RCznj4pefov.

This example shows how international organizations such as the United Nations use their power and influence to spread the pro-abortion agenda all over the globe, especially in the developing world. Disregarding cultural and religious views and values, they demand that developing countries show their commitment to their version of progress by the legalization of abortion.

In their statements, such organizations promise Africans a decrease not only in clandestine, unsafe abortions but also in maternal mortality, if only they would legalize abortion. Yet there is no evidence that lower maternal mortality results from the legalization of abortion. South Africa, for example, legalized abortion twenty years ago with its Choice on Termination of Pregnancy Act, which was signed into law by President Nelson Mandela. The law has been described by the Guttmacher Institute as "one of the most liberal abortion laws in the world".[13] In spite of how liberal this abortion law is, it has been an empty promise to the people of South Africa, as they still have a very high maternal mortality rate of 138 per 100,000 live births, which is even higher than that of Botswana (129 per 100,000 live births), a much smaller and poorer country without legal abortion.[14]

Legal abortion in South Africa has also failed to eradicate the clandestine abortion industry that is thriving across the country. In South Africa abortion is not only legal but also free at public healthcare facilities. But freelance writer Sian Ferguson wrote: "Despite this, illegal abortion

[13] Frances A. Althaus, "Work in Progress: The Expansion of Access to Abortion Services in South Africa Following Legalization", *International Family Planning Perspectives* 26, no. 2 (2000): 84–86.

[14] Central Intelligence Agency, *The World Factbook* (Washington, D.C.: Central Intelligence Agency, 2017), "South Africa: People and Society", https://www.cia.gov/library/publications/the-world-factbook/geos/sf.html.

is surprisingly common. Leading Safe Choices, an initiative by the Royal College of Obstetricians & Gynecologists, estimates that about half of all abortions in South Africa are illegal—although accurate figures are difficult to obtain, because few people admit to having illegal abortions."[15] With the highest GDP on the continent, South Africa is the most developed African country, and for two decades it has offered free legal abortions; yet half of all abortions being performed in the country are illegal.

Meanwhile, the number of registered abortions in South Africa has skyrocketed: from 26,519 abortions in 1997, to 40,353 in 1998, to 89,126 in 2014. These numbers reflect a fourfold increase in abortions within twenty years.[16] Also shocking is the fact that 60 percent of all abortions in South African state hospitals are performed on teenagers. South African Health Department spokesman Joe Maila said about this terrible trend, "More teenagers are having abortions and the numbers are scary."[17]

The "pass the abortion bill" policy that powerful countries have recommended for Africa is not resulting in greater health and happiness for African women. That is why the only ones who rejoice over the spread of abortion in Africa are the pro-abortion organizations funded by the new colonizers. Take, for example, this quote from an Ipas policy director after the passage of the Sierra Leone abortion bill:

[15] Sian Ferguson, "Abortion Is Legal in South Africa—But Illegal Clinics Are Thriving. Why?", April 3, 2017, https://brightthemag.com/abortion-in-south-africa-is-legal-but-half-are-done-illegally-why-969ffcb7dfea.

[16] Wm. Robert Johnston, "Historical Abortion Statistics, South Africa", Johnston's Archive, last updated February 23, 2017, http://www.johnston sarchive.net/policy/abortion/ab-southafrica.html.

[17] Reabetswe Khoabane, "Teenage Abortion Numbers Shoot Up", Times, August 6, 2014, posted at Board of Healthcare Funders of Southern Africa, August 7, 2014, http://ftp.bhfglobal.com/teenage-abortion-numbers-shoot.

This news makes Sierra Leone a real leader in the growing trend of progressive abortion law reform in Africa. With Mozambique's law reform of last year and efforts in other countries to review their restrictive laws, we are seeing great progress toward respecting women's reproductive rights and protecting their health in the region.[18]

The feminist organization FEMNET also celebrated:

Again, we celebrate and congratulate the Parliament for its strong and clear steps to protect women's health and dignity. Sierra Leone stands as a champion within Africa for women's health and rights and a model for numerous other countries that are unwilling to take this bold and important step for what is good and right.[19]

The women of Sierra Leone, however, did not see legal abortion as a "step for what is good and right". Rather, those who were present outside the parliament when the bill was passed expressed profound disappointment in the new law, saying that they were mothers who could never encourage their children to commit abortion. "Our religions do not permit such practice," one woman said, "so also with our culture."[20] Some of the women were given T-shirts to wear and Ipas banners to carry without knowing that they were being used as visual props by the

[18] "Sierra Leone Votes to Reform Abortion Law", Ipas, December 8, 2015, http://www.ipas.org/en/News/2015/December/Sierra-Leone-Parliament -votes-to-reform-abortion-law.aspx?m=1.

[19] African Women's Development and Communication Network, http:// femnet.org/2016/02/09/womensrights-safeabortion-srhr-sierra-leone-safe -abortion-bill-sign-on-online-letter-to-petition-parliament-2/

[20] Edna Smalle, "Sierra Leone News: Parliament Passes Abortion Bill into Law", *Awoko*, December 9, 2015, http://awoko.org/2015/12/09/sierra-leone -news-parliament-passes-abortion-bill-into-law/.

pro-abortion activists. Only after the bill passed did they realize that the "Child Bearing by Choice and Not by Force" inscription on their free T-shirts meant "Death to unborn babies" or "Abortion on demand without apologies". One woman said regretfully, "We were deceived today; we were given T-shirts to come here without being rightly informed on the occasion."[21]

Yes, as mentioned previously, abortion is pushed in Africa by deception and stealth, but when the people discover the truth about the pro-abortion laws being passed in their countries, they fight valiantly to defend the sanctity of every member of their society. As in Imo, Nigeria, religious leaders in Sierra Leone appealed to the government to reverse the pro-abortion law. The Inter-Religious Council of Sierra Leone (IRCSL), which is made up of all the country's religious leaders, went directly to President Ernest Koroma to demand that he not sign the abortion bill. Bishop J. Archibald Cole, president of the Pentecostal Fellowship of Sierra Leone, told Koroma, "We are dealing with the inalienable life of man to live. A bill that would tend to take that life will have serious implications for our generational landscape." The president responded, "Religious leaders represent a huge constituency across the country. I will ask parliament to put a hold on the bill pending discussions on the issue. I will not give assent now but will send it back to parliament."[22]

As hell hath no fury like a feminist who has failed in her single-minded mission to spread abortion, since the president's decision to halt the abortion bill, the government of

[21] Ibid.

[22] State House Communication Unit, "President Koroma Engages Religious Leaders on Abortion Bill", State House, the Republic of Sierra Leone, January 6, 2016, http://www.statehouse.gov.sl/index.php/contact/1416-president-koroma-engages-religious-leaders-on-abortion-bill-.

Sierra Leone has been inundated with petitions, complaints, and statements from foreign organizations demanding the legalization of abortion.[23] Additionally, United Nations experts and the African Commission on Human and Peoples' Rights urged President Koroma to sign the 2015 abortion bill "without further delay". They also called on Sierra Leone "to respect its obligations under international and regional human rights law by ensuring access to sexual and reproductive health and rights for women, including maternal health care and access to all methods of contraception."[24] In this case, we again see that the experts in the halls of Western power disregard the views and the values of an entire nation in order to push their pro-abortion agenda. As of 2017, President Koroma has resisted this foreign pressure and has not signed the abortion bill into law.

The Harsh Reality of Illegal Abortion in Africa

As we have seen, one of the primary arguments used to push the legalization of abortion in Africa is the need to reduce unsafe illegal abortions. Though numbers are

---

[23] For an example of a petition, see Ipas Africa Alliance, "#womensrights #safeabortion #srhr Sierra Leone Safe Abortion Bill: SIGN-ON Online Letter to Petition Parliament", FEMNET, January 14, 2016, https://femnet.wordpress .com/category/power/. For a complaint, see Liz Ford, "Sierra Leone's President Urged to Sign Safe Abortion Bill", *Guardian*, February 3, 2016, https:// www.theguardian.com/global-development/2016/feb/03/sierra-leone -president-urged-to-sign-safe-abortion-bill. For statements, see Marie Stopes Sierra Leone, *Call to Action: Pass Sierra Leone's Safe Abortion Act*, http://www .mamaye.org/sites/default/files/SL%20Briefing%20SA%20Act(1).pdf.

[24] United Nations Human Rights, Office of the High Commissioner, "UN and African Experts Urge Sierra Leone's President to Save Millions of Women's Lives by Signing the 2015 Safe Abortion Bill", http://www.ohchr.org/EN /NewsEvents/Pages/DisplayNews.aspx?NewsID=16994&LangID=E.

difficult to estimate accurately, unacceptably high numbers of illegal abortions are performed across the continent. The typical narrative that abortion proponents offer is that most illegal abortions in Africa are performed by quacks and frauds and are therefore unsafe. But, in reality, many medical doctors generate wealth for themselves through illegal abortions, as did a Sudanese gynecologist who in 2011 finished serving five years in prison for performing illegal abortions in his country. On his release, he was lionized and celebrated in the Netherlands, where he was interviewed on the radio. On the air he said, "I don't regret what I have done for a moment. The years I spent in the prison are the price for saving the lives of thousands of girls and protecting their families. I am fully satisfied, both morally and professionally."[25] So this doctor is a hero, according to pro-abortion Westerners, but what would they think of Dr. Paul Mugahi and Dr. Betty Halivura, who were caught in Kenya in 2016 while performing an abortion on a fourteen-year-old they had kidnapped? They were allegedly working under the instructions of Dr. Halivura's thirty-five-year-old brother, who was reportedly responsible for the girl's pregnancy.[26]

A Nagging Question

Unfortunately, both legal and illegal abortions are occurring throughout Africa. We therefore must ask why African women whose religion and culture cherish children

[25] "Jailed for abortion in Sudan: No regrets", Radio Netherlands Worldwide, https://www.rnw.org/archive/jailed-abortion-sudan-no-regrets.
[26] Paul Amisi, "Doctors Caught Performing Abortion on Kidnapped Girl", Kenyans.co.ke, June 22, 2016, https://www.kenyans.co.ke/news/doctors-caught-performing-abortion-kidnapped-girl.

seek abortions. The sad reality is that the path to abortion is usually paved with anguished tears.

Very often abandonment, pressure, or even threats by the child's father motivate a woman to abort their child. In such a case, the woman might even fear for her life, as there have been instances in which the father of an unborn child killed the mother for refusing to have an abortion. For example, in 2016, in Kenya, a college student was found murdered in her house. Her sister accused the victim's boyfriend of the crime, saying that he killed her because she refused to have an abortion.[27] In a similar show of rage, in Nigeria, Stephen Luka attacked and killed the sister of Justina Dusu, his twenty-seven-year-old girlfriend. After Dusu told her boyfriend that she was pregnant, he asked her to get an abortion, which she refused to do. Later, when she again went to talk with him about the pregnancy, she brought her sister along. "My sister stepped out to receive a phone [call]," she said, "but before she returned, he started hitting me on my head. When I started screaming, my sister tried to enter, but he locked the door. She forced the door open and he descended on her with a machete and killed her."[28]

Sometimes the woman seeking an abortion has engaged in extramarital sex and either she or the child's father feels that the baby must be eliminated in order to avoid responsibility, shame, or punishment. Sometimes the woman seeking an abortion is being sexually exploited as a prostitute, sometimes even against her will. In short, in many cases

---

[27] Margaret Kabiu, "College Student Murdered by Boyfriend over Abortion Differences", April 11, 2016, *Hivisasa*, http://www.hivisasa.com/posts/college-student-murdered-by-boyfriend-over-abortion-differences.

[28] "My Boyfriend Killed My Sister, Rains Abuses on Me, for Refusing Abortion", *Vanguard*, February 10, 2017, http://www.vanguardngr.com/2017/02/boyfriend-killed-sister-rains-abuses-refusing-abortion-woman/.

of abortion, there is a woman in a desperate situation who feels she has no other choice but to kill her child, and this problem is not simply an African one. A study carried out at the Institute for Pregnancy Loss in Jacksonville, Florida, showed that up to 64 percent of post-abortive American women felt pressured by others to have an abortion. In that same study, 67 percent said they received no counseling beforehand, 84 percent reported that they received inadequate counseling beforehand, and 54 percent were not sure about their decision at the time. Some 79 percent were not counseled about alternatives.[29]

The more urgent problem faced by many women in African countries, and in other countries as well, is not that they don't have a legal way to terminate the lives of their unborn children "safely", but that they have too few people who are willing to help them to resist those trying to coerce them into aborting their babies. Such coercion is an all-too-common but unacknowledged form of violence against women.

A pregnant woman deserves better than violent threats and beatings. She deserves better than abortion, another form of violence. She and her unborn child deserve to be loved and cared for. I agree with pro-abortion activists that illegal abortion is a real problem in Africa, but I completely disagree with their proffered solution—to legalize abortion on demand. Making abortion legal will not result in more respect for women. And it might make the choice to bear a child even harder.

If the solution to all of Africa's illegal practices and crimes is to legalize them, then we are a doomed continent.

[29] V. M. Rue et al., "Induced Abortion and Traumatic Stress: A Preliminary Comparison of American and Russian Women", *Medical Science Monitor* 10, no. 10 (October 2004): SR8.

Human trafficking; buying, selling, and consuming illegal addictive drugs; fraudulent financial transactions, computer hacking, identity theft—would legalizing these destructive behaviors improve society? If not, why would legalizing abortion improve the lives of Africans?

And if illegal abortions are so terrible, why do our civil authorities do so little to stop them? Illegal abortions are carried out with impunity because no one is making a real effort to stop them. No one is giving passionate speeches against them at the United Nations or donating funds specifically to train dedicated task forces to go after them.

Law-enforcement agencies in Africa are spread thin, but in some countries they nevertheless make an effort to stop illegal abortions. In February 2016, Dr. Ismail Shamim was arrested in South Sudan after a woman confessed that her daughter had procured an abortion at his clinic. When the South Sudan police raided the clinic, one of the laboratory technicians there said that most of the young women who came in for abortions were secondary school students.[30]

Abortion advocates try to make the case for legalizing abortion in every African country by pointing to unsafe illegal abortion practices, but I would rather harken to the profound words of American columnist and radio talk-show host Dennis Prager, who has pointed out with regard to legal abortion: "Good societies can survive people doing immoral things. But a good society cannot survive if it calls immoral things moral."[31]

[30] Lioto Samuel Raymond, "Doctor Arrested for Conducting Abortions", Gurtong, February 22, 2016, http://www.gurtong.net/ECM/Editorial/tabid /124/ctl/ArticleView/mid/519/articleId/18648/Doctor-Arrested-For -Conducting-Abortions.aspx.

[31] Dennis Prager, "The Most Important Question about Abortion" (transcript of Prager U. course, August 17, 2015), https://www.prageru.com/sites /default/files/courses/transcripts/prager-the_most_important_question_about _abortion-transcript.pdf.

The average person in Africa would say that abortion is unacceptable because it kills a precious unborn child. Many Africans believe that bloodlines date back many generations and stretch forth many generations. For them, even the tiniest unborn baby carries important bloodlines. For them, blood is thicker than water, and so the baby in the womb is the child of someone and the grandchild of someone. For them, it is a real desecration for that blood to be spilled at the hands of an abortionist. An overwhelming majority of Africans say that abortion is intolerable, whether legal or illegal. It is time for the international community to listen to the voices of the African people and to desist from pushing abortion on them.

5

The Normalization of Homosexuality

Male and Female: Made for Marriage

For my people, the Igbos, the *igba ngwu* wedding ceremony precedes any vows that might be said by a Christian
couple in a church. During this traditional ceremony, following family negotiations and agreements, a man and a
woman are joined as husband and wife in the eyes of their
kin and community. The ceremony is picturesque in every
way and so brings to life everything the world roman-
ticizes about Africa—from the kola nuts to the freshly
tapped palm wine, from the colorful attires to the skilled
drummers and agile dancers moving perfectly to the beat.

No doubt many Western elites would enjoy attending
this event, which is so richly and unabashedly ethnic. When
they tout the merits of cultural diversity, they mean native
languages, food, clothing, music, and dance. If they knew
the core reasons for our *igba ngwu* ceremony, however,
they would very likely be repulsed, because their tolerance
of African cultural heritage does not extend to the deepest
thoughts and convictions of Africans. While they might enjoy the catchy beats of membrane drums, they might not
enjoy the final benedictions of the father of the bride as he
publicly prays for the newlyweds, that they might enjoy
not only *ogolo ndu* (long life), *ahu isike* (good health), *udo*
(peace), and *oñu* (happiness) but also *omumu* (fertility).

The Igbo people are not ambiguous about the reason for a man and a woman to unite themselves in marriage. Fertility is considered central, so the entire village publicly prays for it right from the start of a marriage. The very existence and preservation of their bloodlines depend on the fruitfulness of marriages. The procreative purpose of sexuality is the foundation of our families, kindreds, villages, and societies. For Africans, "male" and "female" are not fluid concepts. Sexual differentiation is not an open-ended consideration. Therefore, the meaning and purpose of sexuality cannot be redefined.

In my tribal language, the expression for the sexual act is *mmeko nwoke na nwanyi*, which translates directly as "sexual intercourse between a man and a woman". A similar correspondence is found in other African tongues. There simply cannot be an *igba ngwu* between two women; there cannot be prayers for fertility upon two men. To persuade Africans otherwise, to convince them that marriage and sex are even possible between two women or two men, would require destroying their language and their culture. Such an undertaking is exactly what homosexual activists are attempting in Africa.

The (De)construction Site—Work in Progress

Every design, good or bad, starts in the mind of the designer, every building arises first in the imagination of the architect, and every sculpture is conceived in the creative thought of the sculptor. It is becoming increasingly evident that a new design for mankind has been hatched in the imagination of the wealthiest class of social engineers and cultural architects in the Western world. The most terrifying and disconcerting thing about their design for the human race is that it requires the destruction of everything men and women have held dear for millennia.

The 2015 ruling by the United States Supreme Court that established a civil right to homosexual "marriage" reflected a tectonic shift in the understanding of marriage in America. The victory cries of homosexual-rights advocates resounded throughout the world, for they knew that it was only a matter of time before their radical redefinition of marriage would be imposed everywhere. In Europe, for example, leaders are declaring, in an almost dictatorial manner, that marriage and family structure must be reconfigured in any country that belongs to or wishes to belong to the European Union. In a seemingly synchronized fashion, Western heads of state have made public commitments to promote the normalization of homosexuality and to demolish the bedrock of all known civilizations: the family—a man and a woman, united in marriage, who raise their children in the stable environment created by their commitment to each other. The world is witnessing an effort to reshape society with judicial sledgehammers, legislative chainsaws, and executive bulldozers that are tearing down the meaning and the purpose of male and female and replacing them with gender fluidity and interchangeability, an illusion that is encouraged by artificial reproductive techniques. As modern politicians redesign society, they show themselves to be ever more totalitarian and tyrannical as their tolerance for dissent and resistance declines day by day.

What will become of Africa as the social engineers attempt to redesign the human race? Will Africa be chopped off, knocked down, or just reconditioned to accept the new definitions of "male", "female", and "marriage"? Will African nations be punished into submission, as are increasing numbers of men and women who have voiced their concerns or objections in Europe and America?

During his 2013 visit to Senegal, United States President
Barack Obama commented about the need to treat everyone as equals, especially in national policies and laws. He
could have mentioned the women living in difficult cir-
cumstances across the continent or the plight of the poorest of the poor or the abhorrent caste systems or the deep
racial and ethnic divides causing tension in many African
countries. But, as serious as these problems are, it was very
clear that President Obama had in mind only one issue—
the normalization of the homosexual lifestyle in Africa. He
made specific reference to the efforts his administration
had made to legitimize homosexuality and told Africans to
follow its example by decriminalizing homosexual acts.[1] In
other words, the most powerful leader of the free world
was asking Africans to pick up their judicial sledgehammers and executive hacksaws to deconstruct marriage in
their countries.

The response to this speech was immediate and unanimous, as Mackay Sall, president of Senegal, retorted that
his country was not "homophobic".[2] Everyone, including
President Sall, understands that the first strategy of the pro-
homosexuality crowd is to hang a large label around the
necks of those who refuse to accept their vision of reality.

Many other Africans fearlessly spoke up against President Obama's comment by reaffirming their unwavering
commitment to stable family life firmly embedded in a
healthy marriage culture. This reaction was no surprise,
given the results of the 2013 Pew Research survey on

---

[1] "Obama Urges Gay Rights in Africa in Trip to Senegal", BBC News, June
27, 2013, http://www.bbc.com/news/world-africa-23078655.

[2] Adam Nossiter, "Senegal Cheers Its President for Standing Up to Obama
on Same-Sex Marriage", New York Times, June 28, 2013, https://nytimes
.com/2013/06/29/world/africa/senegal-cheers-its-president-for-standing-up
-to-obama-on-same-sex-marriage.html.

moral views that was carried out in several countries. Most of the Africans surveyed said that they found homosexual lifestyles to be morally unacceptable: 98 percent of respondents in Ghana, 93 percent of respondents in Uganda, 92 percent of respondents in Tunisia, 88 percent of respondents in Kenya, and 85 percent of respondents in Nigeria all disapproved of homosexual behavior.[3]

In complete agreement with my fellow Africans on this point, I wrote the following open letter to President Obama:

Dear President Obama,

I ask you, sir, with all due respect to your highly esteemed office: What if our African values and religious beliefs teach us to elevate the highest good of the family above sexual gratification? What if African society has been naturally wired to value the awesome wonder of natural conception and birth of children within the loving embrace of marriage? What if the greatest consolation of the African child is the experience of being raised by both a mother and a father?

No child (in any part of the world) deserves to be raised in a motherless or fatherless home, because it is almost always a vicious vortex of emotional trauma and turmoil. Africans know and understand this and as such will stand in defiance of your new design of marriage and family. For us to comply with the draconian demands of your "modern" design will entail completely demolishing our society, which is already afflicted with so many problems.

In some parts of Africa, we are still trying to outlaw odious practices such as female genital mutilation, so please don't try to persuade us to introduce yet another type of mutilation into our society. In many parts of Africa, we

[3] Pew Research Center, "Global Views on Morality" (2013 poll), table of results on views of homosexuality, http://www.pewglobal.org/2014/04/15 /global-morality/table/homosexuality/.

are still trying to recover from the deep wounds inflicted by the aberration of marriage that is polygamous marriage, so please don't tell us to take on yet another aberration of marriage—same-sex marriage. In some other parts of Africa, we are still mourning and counting the graves of young people lost to AIDS—a deadly disease rooted in widespread sexual depravity—so please do not encourage our leaders to enact laws that will raise altars to even more sexual depravity.

Africa wants to walk the path of authentic growth, development, and stability. And this path is not paved in sexual "rights", but rather in authentic rights that promote human flourishing and common good. So, on this note, Africans ask for the friendship of all people of goodwill, including the POTUS and other great leaders in the Western world, provided they do not try to strip our Africa of her dignity, which is rooted in stable family structure; provided they do not ask us to demolish our value system in the face of their new design; and provided they do not ask us to sacrifice the stability of our society at the altar of selfish sexual gratification.[4]

Serving the Truth with Love

The one thing that Western pro-homosexuality advocates do not ever consider is that the African men and women who struggle with same-sex attraction are first and foremost the beloved children of Africa. They have mothers, fathers, and siblings who love them. African societies' refusal to redefine the foundation of their civilization does not mean they hate their children who have same-sex

---

[4] Obianuju Ekeocha, "POTUS Take Note: African Views on Marriage", *Catholic Exchange*, July 9, 2013, http://catholicexchange.com/potus-take-note-african-thoughts-on-marriage.

attraction. Rather, it means that Africans want a more profound way of showing their love for their children without
indulging their every wish and desire. Families want truth
balanced by love, and societies want justice evened out
by mercy.

African nations have been labeled as inherently homophobic by Western media. These accusations have been
made on the heels of incidents of mob violence against
homosexuals. Time and time again these cases have been
spun or framed by Western commentators to blame African leaders, both political and religious, for these acts of
violence. In so doing, they have pinned Africans into a
corner: if we don't accept the homosexual lifestyle, we
are homophobic. Thus, many ordinary Africans have been
frightened into silence, because anything less than total
acceptance of homosexual behavior is considered hatred.
We are told that our understanding of human sexuality
and marriage is responsible for the cases of mob violence
against homosexuals. Thus, we try to avoid airing our
opinion about marriage, because no matter how carefully we word this opinion, it has been declared unfit for
public consumption.

But am I a hater for believing that a child should not be
subjected to fatherlessness by the choice of two women?
Am I a bigot for thinking that it is wrong for homosexuals
to exploit poor women through surrogacy? Am I a homo-
phobe for seeing the biological fact that a procreative marital act can be accomplished only by a man and a woman?
No, I am none of these things. Neither I nor anyone in my
sphere of family or friends would ever condone or perpe-
trate an attack on a homosexual.

Attacks against gays are usually carried out by a mob, and
every one of these vicious attacks should be denounced.
What is often not mentioned in the news, however, is that

in many parts of Africa, vigilantism, or mob justice, is a real problem and a cause for worry for everyone, not only homosexuals. This failure of justice in African societies is being used by Western commentators to declare that the African people themselves are the greatest homophobes on the planet, without ever mentioning that mobs are often whipped into violent frenzy for any number of reasons.

In 2011, the Kenyan police for the first time included "lynching" in its crime statistics. The officials recorded 543 victims. In Uganda, 582 people died as a result of lynching in 2014. According to the United Nations, mobs brutally killed 16 people within a month in Malawi. In South Africa, several times a year a person is "necklaced"; that is, he is tied up, and a tire soaked in gasoline is hung around his neck and set on fire. These victims range from people caught in petty crimes to drivers who accidentally knock down pedestrians. Even politicians are not spared, as a furious crowd once dragged the Nigerian lawmaker Bukalo Saraki to a marketplace in the capital, Abuja. The mob ripped off his clothes and hurled insults at him. The reason for the attack was that messages circulating on social media claimed that the senator had illegally enriched himself.[5] If he had been a homosexual, perhaps the story would have made international news.

Nations have the right to establish laws that they believe necessary for social order, and these include laws pertaining to marriage. And parents have the right to teach their cherished beliefs and traditions about marriage to their children. What Africa needs is a better and clearer way of

---

[5] Theresa Krinninger, "Mob Justice in Africa: Why People Take the Law into Their Own Hands", Deutsche Welle, May 5, 2016, http://m.dw.com /en/mob-justice-in-africa-why-people-take-the-law-into-their-own-hands /a-19238120.

conveying their firmly held convictions, of presenting with love the truth as it has been revealed through nature and their culture. Terms such as "defense of marriage" should be used in place of "anti-gay", which can be (and often is) misconstrued as hostility against homosexuals.

But regardless of the language chosen, the leaders and the sexual liberationists of the Western world are working hard to cause an unbridgeable divide between Africans and their culture, between African parents and their same-sex-attracted children, who are hearing from the likes of President Obama that the refusal to redefine African society equates to hatred and discrimination against them.

International Platforms for Propagandas

The United Nations Postal Administration (UNPA) in February 2016 launched a set of six commemorative stamps—two in English, two in French, and two in German—to promote the Free and Equal campaign, which was essentially an effort to legitimize homosexual behavior. The stamps are still being sold at the United Nations headquarters in New York, Geneva, and Vienna.

The permanent missions of Germany, Israel, Netherlands, Norway, the United Kingdom, the United States, Argentina, Australia, Chile, El Salvador, and Uruguay; the delegation of the European Union; and the Office of the High Commissioner for Human Rights, and the UNPA cosponsored the launch of these stamps. According to Sergio Baradat, the artist who designed them, the stamp of a person with butterfly wings represents a transgender person who is "becoming who they really are, blossoming". He added, "We live in a world where even though [developed] nations have embraced marriage equality [and]

LBGT equality, we still have a far, far, far way to go, but we are making some strides."[6]

To the millions of people from countries around the world (especially African countries) where homosexual behavior is considered immoral, the stamps are a form of propaganda from a handful of wealthy countries. This is probably why Usman Sarki, Nigerian ambassador to the United Nations, gave an eloquent rebuke to the organization in anticipation of the roll-out of the stamps celebrating homosexuality and transgenderism. Sarki invoked the United Nations Charter and said that it is the member states that run the United Nations, not the bureaucrats who work for the organization:

> We are distressed and alarmed that the United Nations has adopted an activist stance on a matter that does not enjoy consensus—or, for that matter, majority support among all its member States. What is clear to many is that the UN has now decided without any reservation or hesitation to side with a minority of Member States and practitioners of this lifestyle, in complete disregard of the wishes and concerns of the majority of its member States and the populations that they represent.
>
> It is in that regard that we wish to remind the UN to limit itself strictly to activities mandated by Member States and especially to promote issues that are beneficial to mankind rather than lend itself as tool to promote aberrant behavior under the guise of promoting human rights.
>
> The UN should not take unilateral decisions on such sensitive matters that offend the sensibilities of the majority of its Member States, and contradict their religious beliefs, cultures, traditions and laws. If it must act in this fashion,

---

[6] United Nations, "New Stamps Promoting LGBT Equality Worldwide Unveiled at UN", UN News Centre, February 4, 2016, http://www.un.org /apps/news/story.asp?NewsID=53168#.WSySgzx4WEc.

the UN should promote issues that enjoy consensus and, at the same time, advance the dignity of people and their genuine human rights. In the light of this concern, we call upon the UN not to proceed with this event and to put an end to all processes that are currently in place in all its agencies, funds and programs, that promote and legitimize this tendency on which there is no consensus among member states.[7]

Sarki captures and articulates in his powerful statement the deepest sentiments of the overwhelming majority of the African people. With complete disregard for these people, the pro-LGBT stamps were launched as scheduled.

The Redefinition of Human Rights

To grasp the modern project of the redefinition of human rights, one must look to the United Nations and more specifically to its *Universal Periodic Review* (UN-UPR), which is a mechanism of its Human Rights Council. The UN-UPR was established by the General Assembly in April 2006 for the purpose of regularly examining the human rights performance of all 193 United Nations member states. This peer-monitoring system allows nations to make recommendations to other nations regarding human rights concerns. It would have been a very good accountability mechanism for promoting justice, if only it had not been converted into a platform for globalizing the ideas and the ideologies of a handful of wealthy Western nations.

[7] Austin Ruse, "Nigerian Ambassador Slams UN for Issuing LGBT Postage Stamp", Breitbart, February 4, 2016, http://www.breitbart.com/big -government/2016/02/04/nigerian-ambassador-slams-un-issuing-lgbt -postage-stamp/.

The International Lesbian, Gay, Bisexual, Transgender, and Intersex Association, an advocacy group, referred to the UN-UPR as "the most progressive arena for the protection of the LGBTI community at the international level".[8] This is indeed accurate because within eight years and two review cycles, 158 states received 1,110 recommendations that were specific to sexual orientation, gender identity and expression, and sex characteristics.[9]

Make no mistake: the UN-UPR's adoption of the sexual rights agenda is about naming and shaming those who do not submit to the new definitions of sex and marriage determined by Western elites. Two-thirds of all sexual-rights recommendations were made by countries in the "Western European and Others" regional group, which includes several wealthy countries outside Europe, such as the United States, Canada, and Australia. The most frequently targeted region was Africa, which received over a quarter of all sexual-rights recommendations, including decriminalizing same-sex behavior, recognizing same-sex marriage, allowing the adoption of children by same-sex couples, and redefining the family in law.

In the last two review cycles, twenty-five member countries have accounted for more than 90 percent of sexual-rights pressure from the UN-UPR, with 30 percent of all sexual-rights recommendations coming from just four countries: Canada, the Netherlands, Spain, and France.

[8] Dodo Karsay, Helene Ramos Dos Santos, and Diana Carolina Prado Mosquera, *Sexual Orientation, Gender Identity and Expression, and Sex Characteristics at the Universal Periodic Review* (ARC International, International Bar Association, International Lesbian, Gay, Bisexual, Trans and Intersex Association, 2016) p. 17, http://ilga.org/downloads/SOGIESC_at_UPR_report.pdf.

[9] Daniele Paletta, "New Report Finds UPR Crucial to Protect Human Rights of LGBTI Persons Worldwide", ILGA, November 9, 2016, http://ilga.org/new-report-finds-upr-crucial-to-protect-human-rights-of-lgbti-persons-worldwide/.

THE NORMALIZATION OF HOMOSEXUALITY

Meanwhile, more than 140 member countries have never issued a single sexual-rights recommendation.[10] During the first review cycle, the "Western European and Others" regional group received the fewest recommendations even though it accounted for 76 percent of the recommendations given. The African group, on the other hand, received more recommendations than any other group, but it did not make a single recommendation related to sexual rights. [11]

The sexual-rights recommendations being generated by the UN-UPR demonstrate that the narrative of international human rights law and practice is disproportionately informed by the experiences of Western countries and their domestic and regional paradigms. And this predominance results in the neglect of the views of other nations struggling to participate in international human rights institutions.

Bend, Bow, or Be Broken

Africa's refusal to surrender to the normalization of homosexuality is more adamant now than it ever has been, not because Africans are more opposed to the homosexual

[10] Rebecca Oas, "'Sexual Rights' Proponents Seek Legitimacy through Universal Periodic Review", Center for Family and Human Rights, November 17, 2016, https://c-fam.org/friday_fax/sexual-rights-proponents-seek -legitimacy-through-universal-periodic-review/.

[11] Mari Dahl Schlanbusch, "Sexual Orientation and Gender Identity Rights in the Universal Periodic Review" (master's dissertation, School of Global Studies, University of Gothenburg School of Business and Social Sciences, University of Roehampton Department of Archaeology and Social Anthropology, University of Tromsø, Spring 2013), p. 37, https://www.upr-info.org /sites/default/files/general-document/pdf/-schlanbusch_-_sogi_rights_in_the _upr_-_2013.pdf.

lifestyle than they were before, but because the Western superpowers have rejected sexual differentiation and complementarity, heterosexual marriage, and the traditional family as the cornerstone of their societies. Their embrace of sexual confusion and aberration has caused a chasm between them and Africa, between their culture and ours. In the clashes that have resulted, many Western leaders have revealed themselves to be modern colonial masters, threatening to withdraw aid from countries such as Nigeria and Uganda unless they accept their global sexual agenda.

In 2011 President Obama threatened to cut off foreign aid to Nigeria because its senate passed a bill unfavorable toward homosexuality. Speaking to the Nigerian press about Obama's threat, Zakari Mohammed, a Nigerian lawmaker, said, "We have a culture. We have religious beliefs and we have a tradition. We are black people. We are not white, and so the US cannot impose its culture on us. Same sex marriage is alien to our culture and we can never give it a chance. So if [Western nations] withhold their aid to us, to hell with them."[12] Many Nigerians frowned on the United States' interference in their country's lawmaking process, with many arguing that Nigeria as a sovereign nation has the right to make its own laws without pressure from external forces. "No country has the right to interfere in the way we make our own laws," said Senate President David Mark, "because we don't interfere in the way others make their own laws." Regarding President Obama's direct threat to cut funding, Tosin Omole, a pastor at a church in Lagos, said:

[12] Mfonobong Nsehe, "Obama Fights Nigerian Anti-Gay Bill, Threatens to Cut Off Aid", *Forbes*, December 9, 2011, https://www.forbes.com /sites/mfonobongnsehe/2011/12/09/obama-fights-nigerian-anti-gay-bill -threatens-to-cut-off-aid/#b675cbb4f7bd.

If the US or any other foreign country wants to strip us of aid because we still hold on tightly to our values, then so be it. We are Africans, not Americans. We do not influence other countries when they are making their laws, so it is ridiculous that they'll attempt to influence the way we make our own laws. Africans view homosexuality as immoral. It has never been condoned in Africa, and it will certainly not be tolerated here in Nigeria.[13]

Uganda passed an anti-sodomy law that had prison sentences for, among other things, homosexual acts with minors, homosexual acts when one of the partners is infected with HIV, homosexual acts with the disabled, repeated sexual offenses, and conducting a marriage ceremony for same-sex couples. This law elicited the fiercest outrage from the West, and most commentators in Western media started spreading a rumor that homosexuals were being imprisoned simply for "being gay". This deliberate mischaracterization led to severe penalties for Uganda. The Obama administration issued a strongly worded statement against the country:

> The Department of State is taking measures to prevent entry into the United States by certain Ugandan officials involved in serious human rights abuses, including against LGBT individuals. In addition, the United States will take steps, consistent with current authorities, to prevent entry into the United States by Ugandans who are found responsible for significant public corruption. We are also discontinuing or redirecting funds for certain additional programs involving the Ugandan Police Force, Ministry of Health, and National Public Health Institute, and

[13] Ibid.

cancelling plans to hold a US military-sponsored aviation
exercise in Uganda.[14]

Subsequently, the United States halted $2.4 million in
funding for a Ugandan community policing program. In
addition, Washington shifted some funding for salaries and
travel expenses of Ugandan health ministry employees to
NGOs involved in health programs. It also reallocated
$3 million for a planned national public health institute in
Uganda to another African country and moved a National
Institutes of Health genomics meeting from Uganda to
South Africa, the only African country that has legalized
same-sex "marriage".[15] Other Western countries also
decided either to withhold or to redirect funds earmarked
for Uganda. Among these were the Netherlands, Den-
mark, Sweden, and Norway.[16]

Of all the reactions to the two African nations that
dared to outlaw sodomy, the most pronounced colonial
overreach was the European Parliament's move to suspend Uganda and Nigeria from the Cotonou Agreement,
a treaty between the European Union and the African,
Caribbean, and Pacific Group of States (ACP). In the
motion, the European Parliament stated that it:

[14] Office of the Press Secretary, Statement by NSC spokesperson Caitlin
Hayden on the response to Uganda's enactment of the Anti-Homosexuality
Act, June 19, 2014, https://obamawhitehouse.archives.gov/the-press-office
/2014/06/19/statement-nsc-spokesperson-caitlin-hayden-response-uganda-s
-enactment-an.

[15] Reuters, "U.S. Cuts Aid to Uganda, Cancels Military Exercise over
Anti-Gay Law", June 19, 2014, http://reuters.com/article/idUSKBN0EU26N
20140619.

[16] European Parliament, Motion for a resolution on launching consultations to suspend Uganda and Nigeria from the Cotonou Agreement in
view of recent legislation further criminalizing homosexuality, November 3,
2015, p. 4, http://www.europarl.europa.eu/sides/getDoc.do?pubRef=-//EP
//NONSGML+MOTION+B7-2014-0252+0+DOC+PDF+V0//EN.

firmly condemns the adoption of the "Same-Sex Marriage (Prohibition) Act" in Nigeria and the "Anti-Homosexuality Act" in Uganda; reiterates that these laws constitute grave threats to the universal rights to life, to freedom of expression, of association and assembly and to freedom from torture, cruel, inhuman and degrading treatment; reiterates that sexual orientation and gender identity are matters falling within the remit of individuals' right to privacy, as guaranteed by international law and national constitutions; underlines the fact that LGBTI equality is an undeniable element of fundamental human rights;

Notes that by signing these anti-homosexuality Acts the Governments of Uganda and Nigeria failed to fulfil an obligation stemming from respect for human rights, democratic principles and the rule of law referred to in Article 9(2) of the Cotonou Agreement;

Regrets that all possible options for dialogue under Article 8 of the Cotonou Agreement have been exhausted and notes that they have failed, due to the unilateral refusal on the ACP's side to discuss sexual orientation as a part of the dialogue;

Calls on the European Commission to immediately launch consultations under Article 96 of the Cotonou Agreement with Uganda and Nigeria in view of a possible suspension from the Agreement and to take any appropriate measures while they are conducted;

Urges the European Commission and Member States to review their development cooperation aid strategy with Uganda and Nigeria and to give priority to redirection of aid to civil society and other organisations over suspension—even sectoral—of aid.[17]

This motion is a perfect example of Western colonialism in the twenty-first century. Here the European Union dares

---

[17] European Parliament, Motion for a resolution, p. 5.

to redefine morality and human rights for the rest of the world and to punish any country that disagrees with them.

Bear in mind that the European Union has turned a blind eye to many African dictatorships, rigged elections, unjust imprisonments of political opponents, deeply corrupt governments, and severe human rights abuses. The same Europe has had no problem with funding African leaders who have overstayed the constitutional length of their terms against the will of their people. Yet this same Europe moves to sanction countries based on their cultural understanding of human sexuality.

Regardless of what Europeans and Americans think, homosexuality is one issue that unifies the vast majority of Africans. The African response to the West's bullying on this subject is unanimous and has been summed up by Ofwono Opondo, a Ugandan government spokesman: "Uganda is a sovereign country and can never bow to anybody or be blackmailed by anybody on a decision it took in its interests, even if it involves threats to cut off all financial assistance."[18] So far, the African understanding on the meaning and purpose of human sexuality has not been changed for any amount of euros, dollars, or pounds.

[18] Reuters, "U.S. Cuts Aid".

6

Modern-Day Colonial Masters

The Masters

Half a century after the decolonization of Africa, many older men and women who lived under European rule still think of the colonials as their superiors. I grew up hearing my mum describe the English, without a single hint of irony, as our "colonial masters". And this view made sense to me, because, for almost a century, the English, the French, the Portuguese, and the Spanish ruled, controlled resources, and made important decisions and interventions across Africa. By the time I was born, the influence of these masters had faded into the memories of those who had experienced colonialism.

In the last few decades, however, when each African country is supposedly sovereign and free to celebrate its strengths and traditions, that outside influence has grown increasingly intrusive. Huge moral shifts have occurred in the West, mostly in the sexual sphere, and Western nations are brazenly attempting to impose their new vision of reality on Africa by every means possible. I do not mean to suggest that the rank and file of these nations are trying to remake Africa into their own image. But Western ruling elites, who are privileged, wealthy, and powerful, are indeed behaving as though they are the rightful masters of Africa.

Western governments and organizations sponsor and host meetings, conferences, and summits to discuss African problems. They spearhead extensive contraception programs, HIV-prevention campaigns, youth-empowerment projects, and maternal-health initiatives—all of which are based on the assumption that there are no relevant natural, ethical, or cultural norms for sexual behavior or even fixed biological facts concerning sexual identity. Referring to themselves as experts and champions of human rights, they interfere not only in the domestic affairs and laws of African nations but in their definitions of "man", "woman", "marriage", "child", and "family"—all while claiming to be the disinterested "partners of Africa".

Thus, I call these Western meddlers the "neocolonial masters" of the twenty-first century because, much like the colonials of the nineteenth and twentieth centuries, they have taken strategic positions to advise, direct, persuade, and thereby control other nations and, in the process, destroy the cultures and institutions of the countries they claim to be helping. Of course, these individuals and organizations are doing the same work of deconstruction in their own countries, where they are redefining sexual identity and marriage, for example. But their ambition is not limited to their own nations. No, they wish to recreate the entire world. As the feminists, eugenicists, abortion activists, gender theorists, and sexual revolutionaries attempt to remake reality in most parts of the Western world, they are skillfully imposing their will on Africa too.

The Paternalism and Unsolicited Interventionism at the Root

At any point in history, colonialism has at its roots an interventionism enabled by paternalism. It involves someone intervening in the lives and the decisions of others and claiming that it is for the good and the well-being of the people being colonized. In this way, colonizers take the moral high ground even as they take control of the lives of others.

In the name of "women's rights" or "women's health", Western leaders are quick to name, blame, and shame African leaders at international gatherings for their country's high rates of maternal mortality, teenage pregnancy, illegal abortion, and HIV infection. Cultural conservatism is labeled as the cause of all these woes, and sexual freedom is held up as the solution. Yet, undisciplined sexual behavior, and not cultural norms against it, is the actual cause of ill-timed pregnancies and sexually transmitted diseases, whether in Africa or in the West. In the United States, for example, sexual permissiveness among young people and homosexual men is causing an increase in sexually transmitted diseases, according to statistics collected by the Center for Disease Control:

> In 2014, increases were seen in all three nationally reported STDs. The approximately 1.4 million cases of chlamydia represent the highest number of annual cases of any condition ever reported to CDC. Substantial increases were also seen among reported cases of gonorrhea and syphilis. While young people and women are most severely affected by STDs, increasing rates among men contributed to the overall increase in 2014 across all diseases.[1]

In the United States, the percentage of births to unmarried women has hovered around 40 percent during the last

[1] Centers for Disease Control and Prevention, *Reported STDs in the United States* (Atlanta: Centers for Disease Control and Prevention, 2015), p. 1, https://www.cdc.gov/std/stats14/std-trends-508.pdf.

decade.[2] In Nigeria and Kenya, between 2008 and 2009, it was 6 percent and 19 percent, respectively.[3] Yet American leaders disdainfully encroach on African institutions, finding ways to infiltrate or otherwise influence them in order to establish their own worldview. And when our African leaders resist this overreach, they are punished in the court of world opinion, which is orchestrated by the same people who are trying to control them.

An example of American meddling in Africa can be seen in a 2009 e-mail exchange between Planned Parenthood Federation of America and Secretary of State Hillary Clinton about abortion law in Kenya. Laurie Rubiner, Planned Parenthood's vice president of public policy and advocacy, asked Secretary Clinton to use her influence to stop the Kenyan government from adding a fetal-personhood amendment to its constitution:

> I understand you are going to Kenya next week and while I know the trip is primarily focused on trade issues, I wanted to flag an issue for you because I know it is near and dear to your heart. Kenya has one of the strictest anti-abortion laws in Africa—it is illegal unless a woman's life is at risk and criminalizes both the woman and the provider....
>
> Kenya is restarting a long-stalled constitutional review process and they hope to produce a final Constitution by next year. Religious groups are on a concerted crusade to include new language in the Constitution which would codify that "life begins at conception". The current

[2] Sally C. Curtin, M.A.; Stephanie J. Ventura, M.A.; and Gladys M. Martinez, Ph.D., *Recent Declines in Nonmarital Childbearing in the United States*, NCHS data brief, no. 162, Centers for Disease Control and Prevention, August 2014, https://www.cdc.gov/nchs/data/databriefs/db162.htm.

[3] "Global Children's Trends", The Sustainable Demographic Dividend, http://sustaindemographicdividend.org/articles/international-family-indicators/global-childrens-trends.

Constitution is largely silent on the issue. If this fetal personhood amendment goes forward, it would place Kenya in the small community of nations with such a provision.... For a country trying to regain the momentum of stability and success it enjoyed until recently, such a policy imposition would be a regression for women's rights and for the country writ large.

I went to Kenya last month to work with the coalition that has formed to strategize against the Constitutional amendment and to work toward a less restrictive abortion law. I also visited several of our clinics and providers in Nairobi and in nearby villages where Planned Parenthood has programs to train providers in post abortion care. You have seen this a million times in your travels around the world, so I don't need to tell you how poignant the stories were of the lives saved and lost, the bravery in standing up to constant government harassment, and the fear of what this potential Constitutional amendment will mean to the provision of safe medical services.

I know it is asking a lot, but if there is any way that you could draw attention to this issue when you are in Kenya, you would be even more of my personal hero than you already are. It is our hope that if Kenya knows the world is watching they may be more careful in how they proceed. Of course we would be happy to help you in any way if you decide you want to do something on this while you are there. There is also a Congressional delegation going to Kenya the week of August 8th and we are working on them to have a side meeting on this issue as well.[4]

Clinton's assistant Huma Abedin replied to Rubiner with the following:

---

[4] Laurie Rubiner to Hillary Clinton, July 31, 2009, Unclassified U.S. Department of State Case No. F-2014-20439, Doc. No. C05764008, July 31, 2015, Hillary Clinton Email Archive, Wikileaks, https://wikileaks.org/clinton-emails /emailid/14688.

She isn't doing any specific health or womens events in Kenya but I've also shared your email with policy team at state and embassy staff in Nairobi helping to plan the trip to see if there is any way to address this.[5]

This correspondence is evidence of an attempt by American pro-abortion leaders to manipulate the democratic process in Kenya, and it is not the only proof. According to the United States Government Accountability Office, between 2008 and 2010, the American government funded the International Development Law Organization (IDLO) to provide technical assistance to the Kenyan Committee of Experts, which was the entity drafting Kenya's constitution. The IDLO advised the committee to insert that "the fetus lacks constitutional standing, and that the rights of women under these articles therefore take priority."[6] The IDLO provided examples of countries whose courts have held that fetal rights serve as a partial barrier to the ability of national legislatures to "protect the right to reproductive dignity" via abortion. Their report stated:

> Given the *de facto* decriminalization of access to abortion in Kenya, and the health risks to women in Kenya associated with the current system of abortion provision, and the absence of any express intention to disturb the current situation, it also seems quite feasible that in the coming years, the Kenyan Parliament may wish to take such measures. One way to handle this would be to modify [the constitution] to make clear that a person is a human being who has been born.[7]

[5] Huma Abedin to Laurie Rubiner, July 31, 2009, in ibid.
[6] United States Government Accountability Office, *Clearer Guidance Needed on Compliance Overseas with Legislation Prohibiting Abortion-Related Lobbying* (Washington, D.C.: U.S. Government Accountability Office, 2011), p. 11, http://www.gao.gov/assets/590/585758.pdf.
[7] Quoted in ibid., p. 12.

After all was said and done, the efforts to keep the protection of the unborn out of the Kenyan constitution failed because the final version promulgated on August 27, 2010, states:

1. Every person has the right to life.
2. The life of a person begins at conception.
3. A person shall not be deprived of life intentionally, except to the extent authorised by this Constitution or other written law.
4. Abortion is not permitted unless, in the opinion of a trained health professional, there is need for emergency treatment, or the life or health of the mother is in danger, or if permitted by any other written law.[8]

When calling on favors and twisting arms do not work, our modern-day colonial masters resort to dragging African leadership into expensive legal battles. In 2015, when the Kenyan government decided to prohibit abortion training for healthcare workers, the director of medical services revoked the national abortion-training manual *Guidelines for Reducing Morbidity and Mortality from Unsafe Abortion*. In retaliation, the Center for Reproductive Rights (CRR), an organization founded in America and headquartered in New York, filed a lawsuit against the Kenyan attorney general, the Ministry of Health, and the director of medical services. Their African regional director accused the Kenyan government of allowing thousands of women in Kenya to die or to suffer severe complications needlessly from "unsafe" abortion:

---

[8] Constitution of Kenya (Nairobi: National Council for Law Reporting, 2010), p. 23, http://www.icla.up.ac.za/images/constitutions/kenya_constitution .pdf.

The deaths and injuries of these women can be prevented and must be prevented. Medical professionals in Kenya must be trained and given clear standards and guidelines on providing women who qualify for services and need to end a pregnancy with safe, legal care.

Denying a woman access to the critical health care she needs can lead to devastating consequences in her life, her family, her community, and Kenyan society as a whole.

It is time for the Ministry of Health to take decisive action to protect the health, lives, families, and future of Kenyan women before more women are needlessly harmed by its policies.[9]

The CRR filed the suit on behalf of the Federation of Women Lawyers–Kenya, two community human rights mobilizers, an adolescent rape survivor suffering from kidney failure and other health complications due to an unsafe abortion, and all Kenyan women of reproductive age. One cannot help but wonder how an American pro-abortion organization became an advocate for "all Kenyan women of reproductive age". It seems a classic case of unsolicited interventionism enabled by paternalism.

Extremism of Neocolonial Masters

Some of the most prominent donors that partner with African countries "for the good of Africans" are state-sponsored international development agencies. They include the United States Agency for International Development, the United Kingdom Department for International

[9] Center for Reproductive Rights, "Kenyan Women Denied Safe, Legal Abortion Services", press release, June 29, 2015, https://www.reproductive rights.org/press-room/kenyan-women-denied-safe-legal-abortion-services.

Development, Global Affairs Canada, Agence Française de Développement, the Norwegian Agency for Development Cooperation, the Swedish International Development Cooperation Agency, the Deutsche Gesellschaft für Internationale Zusammenarbeit, and the European Commission's Directorate-General for International Cooperation and Development. By nature these agencies are neutral, and they have provided much help across Africa by supporting agricultural productivity, initiating educational improvements, fighting endemic diseases such as malaria, promoting the ideals of good governance, and leading the response in times of humanitarian crises. But the political priorities of Western governments, and therefore the projects they fund through these agencies, are determined by the current ideological bent of their leaders.

Take, for example, the twists and turns of the Mexico City Policy of the United States. Originally crafted in 1984 by the administration of President Ronald Reagan, it required NGOs receiving American funding to agree that they would neither perform nor actively promote abortion as a method of family planning in other nations. This executive order stopped the flow of federal funds to the abortion-promoting IPPF and MSI. President Bill Clinton rescinded the Mexico City Policy at the beginning of his first term, and President George Bush reinstated it. President Barack Obama rescinded the policy, and President Donald Trump reinstated it again in 2017.

An overwhelming majority of American taxpayers, whether Republican or Democrat, support the core principle of the Mexico City Policy. In a comprehensive Knights of Columbus–Marist poll released in January 2017, 83 percent of those surveyed said they opposed federal funding of overseas abortions. Most revealing about this poll was that 70 percent of the respondents who identified as pro-choice or Democrat said they opposed the use of tax dollars to pay for abortions in other countries.[10]

Given that a significant proportion of Americans are against funding abortions overseas and that many people in the developing world do not want foreign funding for abortions in their countries, the Mexico City Policy is reasonable; but these commonsense considerations have never stopped pro-abortion presidents from promoting and exporting their worldview under the labels of "women's healthcare", "international development", and "humanitarian aid".

When President Trump reinstated the Mexico City Policy in 2017, a number of Western leaders scrambled to make up for the $600 million that America was going to withhold from pro-abortion organizations. They raised about $190 million through the SheDecides campaign, launched in Brussels, where Sweden, Finland, and Canada each pledged $20 million for abortion providers, and Belgium, Denmark, the Netherlands, and Norway each promised $10 million. Absent from the list of donor countries was the United Kingdom, although its minister for international development said that her country already will be spending $200 million on family-planning programs. Private individuals and organizations also contributed to the campaign. An anonymous donor in the United Sates committed $50 million, the Bill and Melinda Gates Foundation promised $20 million, and hedge fund manager and philanthropist Chris Hohn promised $10 million.[11] On

[10] Marist College Institute for Public Opinion, *Americans Opinions on Abortion* (Knights of Columbus–Marist poll, January 2017), p. 8, http://www.kofc.org /un/en/resources/communications/american-support-abortion-restriction.pdf.

[11] Jennifer Rankin and Jessica Elgot, "UK Fails to Contribute as Donors Unite to Bridge US 'Global Gag' Funding Shortfall", *Guardian*, March 2, 2017, https://www.theguardian.com/global-development/2017/mar/02/uk-donors -unite-us-global-gag-rule-shortfall-trump-she-decides-conference-brussels.

top of Canada's commitment to SheDecides, a few days after the Brussels fund-raiser Canadian Prime Minister Justin Trudeau pledged $650 million toward worldwide women's reproductive health programs, including abortion services.[12]

An interesting fact is that those who spend the most to promote abortion in Africa come from countries with low fertility rates. The following donors to SheDecides have fertility rates well below the replacement rate of 2.1 children per woman.

Canada	1.61
Denmark	1.67
Netherlands	1.68
Belgium	1.75
Finland	1.75
Norway	1.75
Sweden	1.89 [13]

Their collective average fertility rate is 1.73, which is almost 20 percent below replacement rate. Without exceptions, these nations are facing the real and imminent threat of a demographic winter, yet they join forces to ensure that the unborn babies of Africa can be aborted without any impediments.

Even though it was mainly for African women, the SheDecides fund-raiser did not make headlines in Africa. No one there was celebrating the money that was raised to abort African children. In fact, Africans were shocked

---

[12] Emma-Louise Boynton, "Justin Trudeau Pledges $650 Million in Funding for Women's Abortion Services Worldwide", *New York Times*, March 10, 2017, https://nytlive.nytimes.com/womenintheworld/2017/03/10/justin-trudeau-pledges-funding-for-womens-abortion-services-worldwide/.

[13] World Bank Database, "Fertility Rate, total (Births per Woman)", http://data.worldbank.org/indicator/SP.DYN.TFR.IN.

to learn that so much money was raised for the sole purpose of facilitating the work of abortion providers across the continent. The message was loud and clear: reducing African population growth is a number-one priority of the West. And why? Because preventing the birth of poor people reduces poverty. Canadian Development Minister Marie-Claude Bibeau explained her government's commitment to "sexual and reproductive health rights" in the following terms: "Contraception and even abortion is only a tool to end poverty.... So we shouldn't look at contraception as the objective. This is not the objective. This is only a tool to reduce poverty and inequality and to make an impact in terms of development and peace and security in the world."[14] It is probably safe to say that this view is shared by many of the Western nations and organizations that contribute millions of dollars to foreign abortions each year.

The Supremacy of Modern Colonialism

For all their talk of equality, Western leaders promoting population control in Africa are demonstrably supremacist toward those who disagree with their views and those who are poorer than they are.

Following the reinstatement of the Mexico City Policy, some NGOs considered changing their policies to exclude abortion from their work in order to qualify for funding from the United States government. In response, the Swedish International Development Cooperation Agency

---

[14]Laura Payton, "Aid Minister Maintains Need for Abortion Rights amid Bishops' Criticism", CTV News, July 11, 2017, http://www.ctvnews .ca/mobile/politics/aid-minister-maintains-need-for-abortion-rights-amid -bishops-criticism-1.3498137.

(Sida) decided to defund any organizations that abide by the Mexico City Policy, saying:

> We have to defend sexual and reproductive health rights and the right to abortion for girls and women in poor countries and when the United States implements a policy that will hit the poorest countries and the most vulnerable groups—women and girls in need of care, Sida has to make sure that Swedish aid continues to go to those activities we have agreed on.[15]

This statement amounts to taking the moral high ground by saying that Sweden is defending the poor of the world against the mean United States. Yet by what means do they defend the poor? By helping them to kill their children.

A more outrageous case of Western supremacy is the anti-carbon campaign launched by Population Matters, an organization based in the United Kingdom. A few days before the 2009 Copenhagen Climate Summit, it launched PopOffsets, a website that enables individuals and organizations to offset their carbon emissions by making online donations for contraception and sterilization in Kenya, Tanzania, Ethiopia, and other developing countries, even though the carbon emissions per capita in the United Kingdom is more than 135 times higher than that in Ethiopia.[16] Go ahead, commandeer the world's resources and live self-indulgently, Population Matters seems to be suggesting, so long as you prevent a poor African from being born.

---

[15] Ben Kentish, "Sweden Vows to Stop Giving Aid to Any Organisations That Follow Donald Trump's Anti-Abortion Rule", *Independent*, July 12, 2017, http://www.independent.co.uk/news/world/europe/sweden-donald-trump -anti-abortion-rule-foreign-aide-ban-mexico-policy-organisations-pro-life -a7837591.html.

[16] "Projects Recently Supported by PopOffsets", PopOffsets, http://www .popoffsets.org/projects.php.

The Infiltration of African Institutions

In addition to expending financial and political capital in
Africa, Western nations and organizations are also infiltrat-
ing African institutions. They are particularly targeting the
educational system, the government, and the media.

The United Nations Educational, Scientific and Cultural
Organization (UNESCO) published a review of sexuality education in eastern and southern African countries in
2013. Given the graphic nature of what the West considers standard sexuality education, the African curricula were
considered weak for a number of reasons: they emphasized
abstinence; lacked adequate information on contraceptives, sex, and sexual health; and excluded key topics such
as reproduction, sexually transmitted diseases, abortion, and
access to contraceptives and sexual health services.[17]

In 2017 the American Guttmacher Institute released a
study on sexuality education in seventy-eight Kenyan secondary schools, and its report lamented that nearly one
in four students in Homa Bay, Mombasa, and Nairobi
counties believes that using a condom during sexual activity is a sign of mistrust. The report bemoaned the finding
that most teachers in these Kenyan schools focus on abstinence as the best or only method to prevent pregnancy.
"A majority of the students we talked to said their teachers
told them that they should not have sex before marriage
and that having sex is dangerous for young people", said
Dr. Estelle Sidze, the lead author of the report. "Fewer
than one in five students said they learned about different contraceptive methods, how to use them and where
to get them, even though equipping adolescents with

---

[17] United Nations Educational, Scientific and Cultural Organization, *Young
People Today. Time to Act Now.* (Paris: UNESCO, 2013), http://unesdoc.unesco
.org/images/0022/002234/223447e.pdf.

this practical knowledge is a crucial component of sexuality education." The report recommended that Kenya add "accurate" and "nonjudgmental" sexuality education, including instructions on how to practice "safe sex", in its life-skills curriculum.[18]

This study of Kenyan schools was initiated and paid for not by the Kenyan government but by the Dutch Ministry of Foreign Affairs and Sida.[19] Nevertheless, the cooperation of the Kenyan government made possible the intrusion into the public schools to conduct the study. African political leaders are easily corrupted by the money offered to them as inducements to go along with such studies. And they too often believe the empty promises of reduced STDs and teenage pregnancies if only they would adopt Western sexuality education. Too often African leaders do not stop to consider that teaching children to have sex at an early age can have only harmful effects, such as the misery of vacuous sexual relationships that most often end in pain and heartbreak, if not in sexually transmitted diseases and unintended pregnancies.

Across Africa, countless government population-control projects have been funded by foreign states and organizations. In 2016 I traveled extensively in Sierra Leone, a scenic country, and I couldn't help but notice the imposing "I am Mr. Condom" billboards set up in every region and province by the Sierra Leone National AIDS Secretariat

---

[18] Estelle M. Sidze et al., *From Paper to Practice: Sexuality Education Policies and Their Implementation in Kenya* (New York: Guttmacher Institute, 2017), p. 8, http://aphrc.org/wp-content/uploads/2017/04/416_Sex-Ed-Policies_Kenya _4.3.17.pdf.

[19] Gustavo Suárez and Carol Gatura, "New Study Shows Sexuality Education Programs in Kenyan Schools Are Failing Students, Falling Short of International Standards", Guttmacher Institute, April 19, 2017, https://www .guttmacher.org/news-release/2017/new-study-shows-sexuality-education -programs-kenyan-schools-are-failing-students.

with the financial support of the United Nations Population Fund (UNFPA) and the Global Fund. I also noticed that these billboards, which probably cost significant sums, were sometimes located in the poorest neighborhoods with impassable roads and dilapidated houses. In their struggle to maneuver through the flooded dirt roads, the people seemed not to notice the billboards that were no doubt targeting them. What a misplacement of priorities! What a waste of limited resources by complicit government ministries and the deep-pocketed Western organizations that spend more money on promoting condoms than on meeting basic human needs!

This sort of waste is very common. In 2016 the Ethiopian government had to destroy sixty-nine million condoms that were paid for by international donors. The condoms were of substandard quality and failed basic elasticity tests. The deputy director of Ethiopia's food and medicine control agency said they also had holes "wide enough to pass liquids through".[20] Thus, $2 million worth of condoms were destroyed in a country where 42.7 percent of the population does not have access to clean drinking water.[21] Imagine the wells and other water projects that could have been funded with that $2 million. Given the magnitude of this misallocation of funds, one wonders whether, apart from contraceptive manufacturers and promoters, anyone really benefits from these programs.

The Western population-control agenda finds its way into Africa not only through funded programs but also

---

[20] Dana Sanchez, "Ethiopia Must Discard 69 Million Defective Donated Condoms", AFK Insider, June 24, 2016 http://afkinsider.com/128609/ethiopia -must-discard-69-million-defective-donated-condoms/.

[21] Central Intelligence Agency, *The World Factbook* (Washington, D.C.: Central Intelligence Agency, 2017), https://www.cia.gov/library/publications/the -world-factbook/geos/et.html.

though the media. The main sources of news for most African leaders and elites are networks such as Cable News Network (CNN). A 2014 report by Ipsos showed CNN to be the leading international news brand in Africa and the Middle East, reaching a larger audience than all their competitors. In Africa, via TV and digital platforms, CNN reaches 71 percent of African business decision makers, 75 percent of high-income earners, and 79 percent of opinion leaders.[22]

CNN has been the subject of allegations of liberal bias by American conservatives, who have complained that the network unfairly covers conservative political candidates and causes. When it comes to issues such as abortion and homosexuality, CNN favors those who promote those behaviors. These allegations are not baseless. In May 2016, CNN CEO Jeff Zucker conceded in an interview that his network has typically leaned to the left. "I think it was a legitimate criticism of CNN that it was a little too liberal", he said.[23]

And how does CNN's "too liberal" bias affect the way it covers population control? Consider, for instance, its favorable report on the launch of Melinda Gates' 2012 contraception campaign, which equates Gates' efforts with female empowerment.[24] Meanwhile, CNN rarely reports on the negative side effects of contraception, the

[22] "CNN Dominates International News Viewership in Africa and Middle East", Screen Africa, August 1, 2014, http://www.screenafrica.com/page /news/television/1644770-CNN-dominates-international-news-viewership -in-Africa-and-Middle-East#.WV5YfYXTWEc.

[23] Becket Adams, "Zucker: Fair to Say CNN Was 'a Little Too Liberal'", Washington Examiner, May 2, 2016, http://www.washingtonexaminer.com /zucker-fair-to-say-cnn-was-a-little-too-liberal/article/2590135.

[24] "Melinda Gates: Give Women the Power to Determine Their Future", CNN, July 9, 2012, http://edition.cnn.com/2012/07/09/opinion/gates -contraception-families/index.html.

fact that hormonal contraceptives do nothing to protect women from sexually transmitted diseases, or the barbarity of abortion procedures. They gave minimal coverage to the 2013 case of Kermit Gosnell, an American abortion provider who was convicted of involuntary manslaughter in the death of a patient and first-degree murder in the deaths of three babies who were born alive during attempted abortion procedures. He was also convicted of hundreds of other abortion-related felony counts. Because this case was barely reported by CNN, few in Africa knew of it.

Another glaring oversight happened in 2015, when a series of undercover investigations exposed the fact that Planned Parenthood abortion providers remove vital organs (lungs, livers, kidneys, etc.) from babies being aborted and illegally sell them. In their coverage of this bombshell exposé, CNN has done everything it can to focus on the way the videos were obtained and to obfuscate the facts in order to shield Planned Parenthood from either criticism or criminal charges.[25]

Growing up in Nigeria, I watched many hours of CNN. I was conditioned to respect and to trust Western news sources and the liberal Western leaders they favored. Bill and Hillary Clinton, Jimmy Carter, Al Gore, Madeleine Albright, and John Kerry—these were shown to be good, selfless, experts and transparent men and women whose chief concern was the betterment of the world. Only in recent years have I come to understand that a network such as CNN could be biased enough to dress up their ideological views as news.

---

[25] Drew Griffin and David Fitzpatrick, "The Real Story behind Those Planned Parenthood Videos", CNN, October 20, 2015, http://edition.cnn.com/2015/10/19/politics/planned-parenthood-videos/index.html.

Through their money and their news media, Western elites are again exerting incredible influence over the people of Africa. Once again, colonial masters are telling Africans that they know best. Only this time around, the very definition of what it means to be a man or a woman or a family is at stake. At the heart of this ideological neocolonialism is Western hypocrisy. Britain and the United States are among the countries that spend the most to undermine African family life and to reduce African fertility, yet they became prosperous and powerful when their laws and policies encouraged the formation of stable, traditional families; their economic booms coincided with population growth. By pushing contraception, abortion, and homosexuality in Africa, Western societies seem not to want Africans to follow the successful responsibility-based approach to human sexuality. Rather, they seem to want Africans to imitate the rights-based approach to sexuality that is causing the demise of Western societies. For Africa to have a promising future, it needs to push back on this flawed paradigm and on the Western influence that is spreading it.

7

Aid Addiction

The Alluring Power of Money

When most people imagine the life of a high-ranking African government official, they probably do not immediately think of shopping trips to London and Paris, holidays in America, birthday parties celebrated in Dubai, real estate in different countries around the world, vacation homes in Western countries, expensive cars, gold and diamond jewelry, and offshore bank accounts. Yet this is a tiny glimpse of the high life of some African elected and appointed government officials, though not all. The African ruling class live like royalty. Their wealth is partly attributable to their salary, which is significantly higher than the national average salary of other professionals in their countries.

Nigerian legislators are among the world's top paid. Between their salaries and bonuses—including allowances for accommodation, vehicle maintenance, personal assistants, house maintenance, domestic staff, entertainment, utility bills, and newspapers[1]—they receive between $150,000 and $190,000 (depending on exchange rates) per year, which is decried by many around the country because

[1] "Nigerian Senators, Reps Earn N6.78 Billion Annually", *Premium Times*, September 4, 2016, http://www.premiumtimesng.com/news/more-news/209789-nigerian-senators-reps-earn-n6-78-billion-annually.html.

minimum-wage workers in Nigeria earn $600 per year
($50 per month). With the exchange rate in 2015, Nigerian
lawmakers earned $189,000, which was considerably higher
than legislators in most developed countries, including,
ironically, legislators from the donor nations that provide
development aid and financial assistance to Nigeria. British
members of Parliament, for example, earn about $105,000,
whereas United States congressmen earn about $174,000.[2]
The average legislators' pay in Nigeria is about 116 times
the national GDP per capita. Kenyan legislators earn about
76 times the national GDP per capita, and Ghanaian legislators almost 30 times national GDP.

Corruption, Mismanagement, and Embezzlement of Funds

One might suppose that, given their wealth, African leaders would be immune to the temptation to gain riches by
illicit or unethical means. But greed knows no bounds,
as can be seen in some famous corruption cases that have
been uncovered by various national anti-corruption organizations. For example, in 2017 Nigeria's Economic and
Financial Crimes Commission accused a former cabinet
member of accumulating $487.5 million in cash and prop-
erties through stolen government funds.[3]

In 2003, former Zambian president Frederick Chiluba
was arrested and charged with stealing and laundering millions of dollars of public money while in office, and this at

---

[2] J.S., L.B., and I.P., "Rewarding Work: A Comparison of Lawmakers'
Pay", *Economist*, July 15, 2013, https://www.economist.com/blogs/graphic
detail/2013/07/daily-chart-12.

[3] Tony Orilade and Aishah Gambari, "Diezani Alison-Madueke: What an
Appetite!" Economic and Financial Crimes Commission, https://efccnigeria
.org/efcc/news/2706-diezani-alison-madueke-what-an-appetite.

a time when the vast majority of Zambians were struggling to live on a dollar a day; many could not afford more than one meal a day.[4] Once feted as a pro-Western, democratic reformer, Chiluba was favored by Western donors. He denied stealing public funds, saying that he had received millions in gifts from corporate interests and well-wishers whose identities he refused to reveal. His case marked a watershed in African judicial accountability: he was the first former president on the continent to be prosecuted for serious crimes. After six years of legal proceedings, he was acquitted of stealing public money.[5] That same year, however, his wife was sentenced to three and half years in prison for receiving stolen government funds.[6]

In another corruption case, former Malawian president Bakili Muluzi was arrested in 2009 for allegedly transferring millions of dollars of donor money to his private account.[7] He was released on bail. As of 2016, the case was still in court.[8] And all the while, Muluzi has continued to serve in government positions.

Losing patience with African corruption, the French government made an unprecedented move in 2012, when it placed three serving Francophone African leaders and their families under investigation for embezzling

[4] David Pallister, "UK Lawyer Helped Zambia Ex-President Launder £23m", *Guardian*, May 4, 2007, https://www.theguardian.com/uk/2007/may/05/world.davidpallister.

[5] Barry Bearak, "Frederick Chiluba, Infamous Zambia Leader, Dies at 68", *New York Times*, June 19, 2011, http://www.nytimes.com/2011/06/20/world/africa/20chiluba.html.

[6] "Regina Chiluba Found Guilty and Sentenced", *Lusaka Times*, March 3, 2009, https://www.lusakatimes.com/2009/03/03/8974/.

[7] "Ex-Malawi Leader on Theft Charges", BBC News, February 27, 2009, http://news.bbc.co.uk/1/hi/world/africa/7912077.stm.

[8] Victor Muisyo, "Malawi: Former President Bakili Muluzi Corruption Trial Drags On", Africa News, June 23, 2016, http://www.africanews.com/2016/06/23/malawi-former-president-bakili-muluzi-corruption-trial-drags-on/.

state funds to acquire luxury assets. The ruling family of Congo-Brazzaville was suspiciously found to have 24 properties in France in their name, 112 bank accounts, and various sports cars—at a time when 70 percent of the people in their country were living on less than a dollar a day. Also under scrutiny was the son of the president of Equatorial Guinea. He owned eleven luxury cars, including a Maserati, a Porsche Carrera, an Aston Martin, a Mercedes Maybach, and two Bugatti Veyrons costing about $1 million apiece. The United States pressed its own case against him, seeking to seize a $38.5 million Gulfstream V private jet, a $30 million mansion in Malibu, and Michael Jackson memorabilia worth $1.8 million. The United States government claimed that these assets had been paid for through corruption.[9]

Malawi became the center of another anti-corruption campaign in 2013, in what is now being called "Cashgate". During a series of police raids, several high-level officials were caught with piles of cash hidden in their homes and cars. Several government figures were arrested and accused of exploiting a loophole in the government's payment system—known as the integrated financial management information system—to divert millions into their own pockets. According to some estimates, the stolen funds totaled $250 million,[10] a significant amount, given that the country's GDP is a mere $5.4 billion.[11]

One of the most egregious examples of African corruption in high places is the late General Sani Abacha, who

---

[9] Angelique Chrisafis, "France Impounds African Autocrats' 'Ill-Gotten Gains'", *Guardian*, February 6, 2012, https://www.theguardian.com/world/2012/feb/06/france-africa-autocrats-corruption-inquiry.

[10] "'Cashgate'—Malawi's Murky Tale of Shooting and Corruption", BBC News, January 27, 2014, http://www.bbc.co.uk/news/world-africa-25912605.

[11] World Bank, Malawi GDP, http://data.worldbank.org/country/malawi.

ruled Nigeria in the nineties and had accrued a staggering
$4 billion fortune by the time he died in 1998.[12] In 2012,
the former Nigerian minister of education Oby Ezekwesili
said that since independence in 1960 Nigeria had lost more
than $400 billion to fraud and corruption.[13]

A similar claim was made in 2016 during the launch of
a corruption awareness campaign by the Nigerian information minister Lai Mohammed, who told reporters that
about $6.8 billion had been stolen from the national coffers
between 2006 and 2013. And he listed those responsible
for this: a number of state governors, ministers, public officials, businessmen, and bankers.[14]

Endemic government corruption is one of the most
debilitating problems impeding the progress of Africans.
Most African countries rank very poorly on the international Corruption Perception Index (CPI). According
to the 2016 CPI, published by Transparency International,
twelve out of the twenty most corrupt countries in the
world are in Africa. Whereas the least corrupt country in
the world had a transparency score of ninety, African countries scored below fifty, with the exception of Botswana,
Cape Verde, Mauritius, Rwanda, and Namibia.[15] Global
Financial Integrity estimated that between 1970 and
2008 Africa lost more than $854 billion in illicit financial

[12] David Pallister and Peter Capella, "British Banks Set to Freeze Dictator's
Millions", *Guardian*, July 7, 2000, https://www.theguardian.com/uk/2000/jul
/08/davidpallister?INTCMP=ILCNETTXT3487.

[13] Ikechukwu Nnochiri, "Nigeria Loses $400bn to Oil Thieves—Ezekwesili",
Vanguard, August 28, 2012, http://www.vanguardngr.com/2012/08/nigeria
-loses-400bn-to-oil-thieves-ezekwesili/.

[14] Afolabi Sotunde, "Nigerian Minister Says $6.8 bn of Public Funds Sto-
len in Seven Years", Reuters, January 19, 2016, http://af.reuters.com/article
/africaTech/idAFKCN0UX0D4?pageNumber=1&virtualBrandChannel=0.

[15] Transparency International, Corruption Perception Index 2016, http://
www.nationsonline.org/oneworld/corruption.htm.

outflows, an amount that far exceeds official aid and development inflows.[16]

The staggering prevalence of corruption makes one wonder why donors keep giving money to African leaders, knowing full well that they will line their pockets with it. Many experts have said that continued support only rewards corruption and might be making it worse. Joseph Hanlon of the Open University wrote: "Donors inveigh against corruption, yet give more aid to corrupt governments. Debate continues on the causes of developing country corruption, but with little consideration of the possibility that the behaviour of donors may unintentionally promote corruption."[17] The statement echoes the wisdom that giving aid to corrupt leaders and expecting them to become honest men is like giving money to a drug user and expecting him to give up his drug habit.

But is it not possible that donors do not care so much about African corruption so long as they get what they really want out of the bargain? Their willingness to give money to corrupt leaders may be matched by the willingness of these leaders to allow a new, ideological colonization of the African people.

High Dependency and Addiction to Aid

How much aid money is being injected into Africa? In the first forty years after independence, Africa received about

---

[16] Dev Kar and Devon Cartwright-Smith, *Illicit Financial Flows from Africa: Hidden Resource for Development* (Washington, D.C.: Global Financial Integrity, 2010), p. 1, http://www.gfintegrity.org/storage/gfip/documents/reports /gfi_africareport_web.pdf.

[17] Joseph Hanlon, "Do Donors Promote Corruption? The Case of Mozambique", *Third World Quarterly* 25, no. 4 (2004): 747–63, http://dx.doi.org /10.1080/01436590410001678960.

$400 billion of aid from the developed world—about six times what the United States pumped into the reconstruction of Western Europe after World War II.[18] Africa receives more than $50 billion from Western donors every year,[19] yet the economic well-being of most Africans has not improved. The per capita GDP of Africans living south of the Sahara declined at an average annual rate of 0.59 percent between 1975 and 2000. Over that period, per capita GDP adjusted for purchasing power parity declined from $1,770 in constant 1995 international dollars to $1,479.[20] Foreign aid to Africa has translated not into better living standards for Africans but into a deepened dependency of African rulers on Western donors. There are many aid-dependent countries in Africa that cannot balance their budgets without donor support. For example, aid makes up about 40 percent of the Malawi national budget. This dependency is what makes African nations so vulnerable and puny in the presence of wealthy donor nations.

In his book *Aid to Africa: Redeemer or Coloniser?* African policy analyst Hakima Abbas described how the dependence of some African countries on aid has led to aid addiction, giving their donors the opportunity to colonize them:

[18] Ross Clark, "Britain Leads the Way in Foreign Aid—Unfortunately", *Express*, June 19, 2013, http://www.express.co.uk/comment/expresscomment /408548/Britain-leads-the-way-in-foreign-aid-unfortunately.

[19] International Development Statistics, database search for official-development-assistance disbursements from all donor countries to all recipients from 2005 to 2015, Organisation for Economic Co-operation and Development, http://stats.oecd.org/qwids/#?x=2&y=6&f=3:51,4:1,1:1,5:3, 7:1&q=3:51+4:1+1::1+5:3+7:1+2:262,240,241,242,243,244,245,246 ,249,248,247,250,251,231+6:2005,2006,2007,2008,2009,2010,2011,2012,2013 ,2014,2015.

[20] Thompson Ayodele et al., *African Perspectives on Aid: Foreign Assistance Will Not Pull Africa Out of Poverty*, Cato Institute, September 14, 2005, https:// www.cato.org/publications/economic-development-bulletin/african -perspectives-aid-foreign-assistance-will-not-pull-africa-out-poverty.

There are African governments that are in effect addicted to donor funds and would not be able to finance their own domestic budgets without any infusion of cash from external actors. Aid has a powerful effect on state institutions in Africa. Aid can therefore become addictive and infect the autonomy of governments. Economic sovereignty in Africa has become co-opted because a significant number of governments rely on foreign official development assistance (ODA) to finance their annual budgets.[21]

For example, according to Abbas, in 2005 the Ugandan government collected only 57 percent of the taxes due from its citizens. Rather than fix whatever the collection problems might be, leaders turn to foreign aid to make up the budget shortfall. With such an easy fix, the state has limited incentive to improve its tax collection. But just as drug addicts will steal food money from their own families to pay their dealers, some African leaders will sacrifice what is in the best interests of their people to please their donors.

Aid sustains several African countries but in doing so it deprives them of the autonomy necessary to make decisions that are genuinely in the interests of their people. This gives donors the power and leverage to direct key aspects of the government's economic and political agenda. This means that African governments can be seen as willing participants in the aid colonisation process. Aid packages tend to be filled with conditionalities that perpetuate a kind of paternalism towards the recipient and undermine its autonomy.[22]

[21] Hakima Abbas and Yves Niyiragira, eds., *Aid to Africa: Redeemer or Coloniser?* (Cape Town, Dakar, Nairobi, and Oxford: Pambazuka Press, 2009), p. 5.
[22] Ibid.

This aid with "conditionalities" is at the core of the ideological neocolonialism taking place across Africa. It explains how philanthropy moguls such as Bill and Melinda Gates can influence, or even direct, the population-control agenda of entire nations and how the wealthy donor nations have become major decision makers in the reproductive lives of millions of African men, women, and children.

The Politics of Aid with Strings Attached

In the not too distant past, reproductive health issues were considered sensitive matters because they are linked to sexuality and sexual behavior. Most cultures throughout the world, and those in Africa are no exception, have deeply rooted mores regarding which sexual behaviors are acceptable and which are not. These mores arose in the prepolitical realms of family and religion, and people who vest moral authority in their traditions, including many Africans, have resisted the attempts to make such matters open to change through public debate and government interference. As a result, Western population-control programs failed to catch on in Africa.

That is, until the developed world adopted a new strategy in its efforts to curb African population growth. In September 1994 the United Nations coordinated an International Conference on Population and Development (ICPD) in Cairo, Egypt, which brought together twenty thousand delegates from various governments, United Nations agencies, and NGOs. At this event the language of sexual and reproductive health was reshaped in terms of human rights, and respect for these newly discovered rights became the criterion for receiving humanitarian assistance.

The outcome document of the ICPD defined reproductive health in this way:

> Reproductive health is a state of complete physical, mental and social well-being and not merely the absence of disease or infirmity, in all matters relating to the reproductive system and to its functions and processes. Reproductive health therefore implies that people are able to have a satisfying and safe sex life and that they have the capability to reproduce and the freedom to decide if, when and how often to do so. Implicit in this last condition are the right of men and women to be informed and to have access to safe, effective, affordable and acceptable methods of family planning of their choice, as well as other methods of their choice for regulation of fertility which are not against the law.[23]

The document also laid the foundation for international donors to become the primary providers of contraceptive drugs and devices in poorer countries:

> Without jeopardising international support for programmes in developing countries, the international community should, upon request, give consideration to the training, technical assistance, short-term contraceptive supply needs and the needs of the countries in transition from centrally managed to market economies, where reproductive health is poor and in some cases deteriorating. Those countries, at the same time, must themselves give higher priority to reproductive health services, including a comprehensive range of contraceptive means,

[23] International Conference on Population and Development, *Programme of Action of the International Conference on Population Development* (New York: United Nations Population Fund, 2014), p. 59, http://www.unfpa.org/sites/default/files/pub-pdf/programme_of_action_Web%20ENGLISH.pdf.

and must address their current reliance on abortion for fertility regulation by meeting the need of women in those countries for better information and more choices on an urgent basis.[24]

The writers of the document apparently anticipated that with more aggressive persuasion campaigns, the demand for contraceptives in the developing world would increase:

> In order to meet the substantial increase in demand for contraceptives over the next decade and beyond, the international community should move, on an immediate basis, to establish an efficient coordination system and global, regional and subregional facilities for the procurement of contraceptives and other commodities essential to reproductive health programmes of developing countries and countries with economies in transition.[25]

This call to action became the rock upon which wealthy Western donors built their population-control fortress. From that point onward, the deep-pocketed international community raised family planning in developing countries to the level of a humanitarian crisis and exponentially increased its spending in this area. According to a report by the UNFPA, in 1993, the year before the Cairo conference, the total amount spent by donors on family planning and population assistance was $610 million. The year after the conference, the amount went up to $1.3 billion, an increase of more than 200 percent.[26] "In sub-Saharan

[24] Ibid., p. 63.
[25] Ibid., p. 69.
[26] United Nations Population Fund, *Financial Resource Flows for Population Activities in 2002* (New York: United Nations Population Fund, 2002), Table 4: Final Donor Expenditures for a Population Assistance, by Channel of Distribution, p. 24, http://www.resourceflows.org/sites/default/files/UNFPA%20 FRFPAR%202002.pdf.

Africa, the NGO channel grew in popularity since 1994 when, with the exception of 1995, it provided the most population assistance."[27]

At the beginning of the new millennium, there was a 50 percent increase in donations to population-control programs. The family-planning expenditures of bilateral organizations, multilateral organizations, and NGOs hit $3.2 billion in 2002, up from $2 billion in 2001.[28] In the same year, private groups such as the Bill and Melinda Gates Foundation, the Rockefeller Foundation, the Hewlett Foundation, and the Packard Foundation together donated more than $400 million, of which the Bill and Melinda Gates Foundation donated 65 percent.[29]

These philanthropic foundations have had a sustained commitment to reducing fertility in poorer countries and have continued to give to this cause, even if it means that much of their money fails to achieve their desired ends. As of 2012, the Gates, Rockefeller, Hewlett, Packard, Ford, and MacArthur Foundations donated more than $480 million, and the Bill and Melinda Gates Foundation donated 86 percent of it.[30] In addition to these private foundations, there are a number of Western nations who support the population-control campaign that was invigorated by the Cairo conference. Together, these nations donate up to 90 percent of all the population assistance given to the developing world. These are the top donor nations of 2012 (in descending order): the United States, the United Kingdom, the Netherlands, Germany, Sweden, France, Norway, Australia, the European Union, and Japan. The United States

[27] Ibid.
[28] Ibid., p. 23.
[29] Ibid., p. 21.
[30] Ibid., p. 21.

gave 57 percent of the total amount that year.[31] The degree
to which the United States has been financing population
control in the developing world helps to explain the shock
waves that were felt by abortion providers when President
Trump reinstated the Mexico City Policy via an executive
order; in the time it took for Trump to tweet a message,
they lost half of their funding.

It is also noteworthy that, of five geographical regions,
sub-Saharan Africa has been the largest recipient of
population-control funds, receiving 71 percent of them in
2012.[32] This was not always the case: in 2002 sub-Saharan
Africa received 46 percent of all donations for population
control, and Asia and the Pacific received 30 percent.[33]
But Africa has been particularly targeted ever since and has
received approximately $72 billion dedicated to popula-
tion control in the last twenty years. What is rather aston-
ishing is that hardly any African leaders have made public
statements that suggest that they question this concerted
attempt to curb the population growth of their countries. It appears that aid money, no matter what strings are
attached to it, is welcome to them.

In the last two decades, the developed world has sent a
staggering $106.2 billion to the developing world in order
to slow its population growth. As a result of the Cairo
Conference call to action, donors have increased their
annual spending on population control of the poor from
$610 million in 1993 to $12.4 billion in 2012, a staggering increase of 1,932 percent.[34] To put this in perspective,
the total amount of foreign aid to the developing world

[31] Ibid., p. 15.
[32] Ibid., p. 22.
[33] Ibid., p. 23.
[34] Ibid., p. 24.

increased from $56 billion in 1993[35] to $133.75 billion in 2012,[36] an increase of 138 percent, which, though high, is dwarfed by the huge increase in population-control funding. In fact, population-program donations to Africa used to be the lowest portion of social-sector foreign aid, much lower than aid for education, health, water, sanitation, and so on. But since 2009, population-control funding has surged ahead of funding for everything else.[37] In 2014, the United States and the United Kingdom targeted 31 percent and 43 percent, respectively, of their African aid to population control.[38] The amounts are significant because these two nations are the highest foreign-aid donors in the world.

Yet ideologically driven advocates keep asking wealthy donors at international gatherings to put even more focus on providing contraceptives for women in the developing world. In 2012, when population-control funding reached the highest it had ever been, Melinda Gates launched her worldwide campaign to "put birth control back on the agenda".[39] Her efforts have been so well received in

[35] United Nations Children's Fund, *The Progress of Nations*, 1995, https://www.unicef.org/pon95/aid-0004.html.

[36] International Development Statistics, database search for official-development-assistance disbursements in all sectors from all donors, in current prices, Organisation for Economic Co-operation and Development, http://stats.oecd.org/qwids/#?x=2&y=6&f=3:51,4:1,1:1,5:3,7:1&q=3:51+4:1+1:1+5:3+7:1+2:262,240,241,242,243,244,245,246,249,248,247,250,251,231+6:2005,2006,2007,2008,2009,2010,2011,2012,2013,2014,2015.

[37] Organisation for Economic Co-operation and Development (hereafter OECD), *Development at a Glance: Statistics by Region*, 2016, p. 13, https://www.oecd.org/dac/stats/documentupload/2%20Africa%20-%20Development%20Aid%20at%20a%20Glance%202016.pdf.

[38] OECD, *Development at a Glance*, p. 12.

[39] TED.com, "Melinda Gates, 'Let's Put Birth Control Back on the Agenda'", published April 11, 2012, TED video, 25:26, https://archive.org/details/MelindaGates_2012X.

the Western world, especially among the humanitarian-aid community, that they have resulted in even more Western spending on family planning for the poor of the world. And there can be no doubt that there are many cooperative and compliant cabinet members, ministers, legislators, government officials, and reproductive-health NGO operatives in the developing world who are bene-fiting from this largesse.

The Failure of Multibillion-Dollar Contraception Interventions

Contraception providers and advocates are quick to declare the successes of their programs to justify their interference in Africa. They conflate the amount of donor-sponsored contraceptives given to the poor with the number of pregnancies that were prevented by them, which is then conflated with the number of "children saved".[40] But in reality, no matter how much money is spent on sending contraceptives to Africa, there is still minimal acceptance of these artificial methods of family planning among Africans.

A number of studies illustrate the lack of African zeal for contraception. One notable phenomenon is the high rate of contraception discontinuation. Lifetime contra-ceptive discontinuation is measured as the percentage of currently married women who used a method of contra-ception in the past but were not using a method at the time of the survey. According to a survey by the United States Agency for International Development (USAID),

[40] Anne Zeiser, "Family Planning Summit Will Save 3 Million Children's Lives by 2020", HuffPost, July 12, 2012, http://m.huffpost.com/us/entry/1663429.

the discontinuation rates in sub-Saharan Africa are the highest in the world. The average discontinuation rate in the eighteen African countries surveyed is 53 percent, much higher than the discontinuation rates in most of Asia and Latin America, which on average are about 30 percent.[41] A majority of the women surveyed gave a fertility-related reason for their discontinuation of contraception. These included concerns about side effects or health risks, infrequent sex, husband was away, became pregnant while using, wanted to become pregnant, or became menopausal. Contrary to the "unmet need" narrative, most women stop using contraception for reasons other than cost or accessibility.[42]

The survey also found that the intention not to use contraception in the future is very high in sub-Saharan Africa. In six of the eighteen countries in this region, at least 50 percent of current nonusers said that they did not intend to use contraception in the future. The authors of the survey described this intention as a "cause for concern". They concluded: "Over time, contraceptive use rates have increased substantially in most countries. However, while contraceptive prevalence rates in some countries in South/Southeast Asia and Latin America and the Caribbean are high and leveling off, prevalence rates in several sub-Saharan countries are low and have remained almost unchanged."[43]

The conclusion matches a 2011 study of family-planning trends in sub-Saharan Africa, where the annual rate of increase in contraceptive use was 1 percent or less

---

[41] Shane Khan et al., *Contraceptive Trends in the Developing World* (Calverton, Md.: Macro International, 2007), p. 59, https://www.dhsprogram.com/pubs /pdf/CR16/CR16.pdf.

[42] Ibid., p. 60.

[43] Ibid., p. 69.

in most of the countries studied, including Côte d'Ivoire, Ethiopia, Tanzania, Cameroon, Uganda, Kenya, Zimbabwe, Burkina Faso, Rwanda, Ghana, Togo, Nigeria, Benin, Guinea, Eritrea, Mali, Senegal, Liberia, Niger, and Chad. More than half of these countries saw an increase of less than 0.5 percent.[44] A report from the United Nations showed a 13 percent increase in contraceptive use in sub-Sharan Africa from 1990 to 2012, which is consistent with a 1 percent annual increase, and a 3 percent decrease of the so-called unmet need for contraception.[45] A decrease in unmet need of less than 3 percent, in spite of an astronomical 1,932 percent increase in donor spending to meet that need, hardly seems worthy of the word "success", unless one applies the word to the those who have been enriched by Western spending—the privileged class of those who promote and administer family-planning programs in Africa. Apparently, like many other Western-initiated aid projects directed toward Africa, population "assistance" has done little more than enrich those at the top of African society.

The real shame, however, is not that $72 billion (over twenty years) failed to prevent a proportionate decrease in the number of Africans born, but that so much money was targeted for that purpose in the first place. To put the amount in perspective, in the last forty years, Africa has received about $400 billion in total aid for economic

---

[44] Mona Sharan et al., "Family Planning Trends in Sub-Saharan Africa: Progress, Prospects, and Lessons Learned", in *Yes Africa Can: Success Stories from a Dynamic Continent*, ed. Punam Chuhan-Pole and Manka Angwafo (Washington, D.C.: World Bank, 2011), 449, http://siteresources.worldbank.org /AFRICAEXT/Resources/258643-1271798012256/YAC_Consolidated _Web.pdf.

[45] United Nations, *The Millennium Development Goals Report 2014* (New York: United Nations, 2014), p. 32, http://www.un.org/millenniumgoals/2014%20 MDG%20report/MDG%202014%20English%20web.pdf.

development, peace and security, education and social services, health care, humanitarian assistance, and ecology.
To spend such a huge amount of this total on contraceptives illustrates the priorities of the donor nations.

Sadly, the African leaders who grow rich through aid or
whose careers are dependent on it are willing to cooper-
ate with the nations and the organizations that are carrying
out a population-control crusade in Africa, an ideological
neocolonialism, no matter what harm it might be causing
Africans. During a private meeting with a high-ranking
government official of an East African country, I shared
my observations of the reproductive-health programs in
her country being financed by Western aid. I showed her
statistics and facts. I had photos of graphic sex-education
programs in rural primary schools. I explained the efforts
being made to legalize abortion. I gave her names, dates,
and locations to corroborate everything I said. She was out-
raged by what I presented; she said that she and most of
her colleagues in government were pro-life and respected
the dignity of human sexuality. But when I asked her to
oppose the organizations that are behind the efforts to undermine the dignity of human life and sexuality, she said
that she could not, because those organizations paid for part
of her department's budget. As she listed all the perks of her
job that were possible only with foreign money, including travel to conferences and meetings around the world, I
came to understand the strength of the grip of aid addiction.

As with other programs in Africa, the primary benefi-
ciaries of foreign-sponsored reproductive-health projects
are the aid addicts within the ranks of government officials.
They are so dependent on donor funds that they cannot
imagine life without them, even when they see the harm
being done by this new colonialism. Aid has become the
opium of the ruling classes of Africa.

8

Toward the Decolonization of Africa

The Cause of Ideological Colonization

For more than a decade, I have worked as a biomedical scientist in pathology. My job entails the analysis of blood cells, too small for the naked eye to see, to diagnose hematological diseases such as anemia, leukemia, and hemophilia. I try to detect abnormal or dysfunctional blood cells that may be the cause of potentially life-threatening diseases. Countless patients have been given urgent, life-saving treatment based on something I or my colleagues discovered. In this line of work it is important to take note of everything and not to miss anything, knowing that a patient's life could be at stake. This experience has convinced me that the first and most important step toward any recovery is to find the root cause of the illness or the abnormality.

Much of this book is, in many ways, a search for the root cause of the ideological colonization of Africa. And this search points to the economic frailty and vulnerability of African nations, which have been brazenly exploited by wealthy ideologues from Western nations and organizations whose thirst for power, it seems, can be slaked only by controlling the destiny of our countries.

Stop the Corruption, Stop the Bleeding

Exposing corruption and aid addiction in African governments was by far the most difficult thing for me to do,
because it was hard to admit that the harm being done to
our cultures and institutions by the new ideological colonization is largely self-inflicted. Fraudulent transfers of
government funds have resulted in huge financial deficien-
cies in our public treasuries. According to the Center for
International Policy, from 1970 to 2008, Africa lost $854
billion in cumulative illicit capital flight, which would
have been enough to wipe out the region's total outstand-
ing external debt and leave $600 billion for poverty alle-
viation and economic growth.[1] No wonder government
leaders try to cover up their thefts by accepting foreign
aid, never mind the strings attached. If Africa cleaned up
its corruption, such aid would not be needed. If it does not
combat corruption, its future will be bleak. The Center
for International Policy concluded that "so long as illicit
capital continues to hemorrhage out of poor African countries over the long term at a rapid pace, efforts to reduce
poverty and boost economic growth will be thwarted as
income distribution becomes ever more skewed leading to
economic and political instability."[2]

Given that deep-seated corruption is part of the root
cause of Africa's problems, it makes no sense for the international community to continue its funding of African
leaders. Many experts have said for many years now that
foreign aid will never be able to pull Africa out of the pit of

[1] Dev Kar and Devon Cartwright-Smith, *Illicit Financial Flows from Africa: Hidden Resource for Development* (Washington, D.C.: Global Financial Integrity, 2010), p. 18, http://www.gfintegrity.org/storage/gfip/documents/reports/gfi _africareport_web.pdf.

[2] Ibid., p. 17.

poverty and stunted economic growth so long as its leaders keep their fingers in the cookie jar. As British economist Peter Bauer said in 1974: "What holds back many poor countries is the people who live there, including their governments. A society which cannot develop without external gifts is altogether unlikely to do so with them."[3]

Foreign aid separates government leaders from their citizens, to whom they are supposed to be accountable. This is the doorway to corruption. In a collaborative essay, development experts Todd Moss, Gunilla Pettersson Gelander, and Nicholas van de Walle argued that nations beholden to donors for most of their revenues have less incentive to be accountable to their citizens than states dependent on domestic tax revenue. They also said that goods provided by donors, such as four-wheel-drive vehicles or "sitting fees" for attending donor seminars (which can exceed the monthly salaries of civil servants), can become objects of political patronage, reinforcing the "patrimonial state" and further undermining the prospects for democracy.[4] Thus, in the quest for decolonization, Africa needs to combat corruption while overcoming aid dependency.

The Truth about Aid

Our giving alms to the poor so that they can feed or clothe their children puts an instant smile on their faces and makes

[3] P. T. Bauer, "Foreign Aid, Forever?", *Encounter* (March 1974): 17, http://www.unz.org/Pub/Encounter-1974mar-00015?View=Overview.

[4] Todd Moss, Gunilla Pettersson Gelander, and Nicolas van de Walle, "An Aid-Institutions Paradox? A Review Essay on Aid Dependency and State Building in Sub-Saharan Africa" (Center for Global Development Working Paper No. 74; Mario Einaudi Center for International Studies Working Paper No. 11-05, January 2006), available at SSRN, http://dx.doi.org/10.2139/ssrn.860826.

us feel good too, for offering relief or even saving lives. But what if we see the same poor beggar every day in the same place for the next twenty years, complaining about the same problems? We might start to wonder whether he is trying to improve his lot in life or is simply living off the charity of others. In some cases, the poor fellow might not be able to make any headway, because of serious and irreversible disabilities. But in other cases, our charity might be enabling bad habits of addiction to drugs or alcohol. If we had real compassion, would we not try to help such a person into a rehab program, so that he could regain his freedom and self-respect?

This analogy applies to foreign aid. Some forms of aid are necessary in order for people to survive disasters, such as earthquakes, famines, or wars. The developed world has been very generous in its relief efforts, which have helped African countries countless times. Such humanitarian aid is laudable. Aid given to education and training programs that give promising young people a future they otherwise would not have had is also commendable. But foreign money that does little more than make aid junkies out of corrupt government officials is of no help at all.

I am an advocate of education because I was born into a family that rose out of poverty by getting hold of an education lifeline. My grandparents came of age in the 1920s, which were the golden years of the colonial era, but they did not have the opportunity to receive an education. My grandfather cultivated and sold coconuts for many years, and his family barely got by on what he made. In 1941, when my father turned seven, my grandfather made a decision that would change the fate of my entire family: he borrowed forty pounds to send my father to school, where he learned to read and write. A new world opened for my father, who eventually received a master's degree in accounting from the University of Cambridge. He never had to sell coconuts for a living; nor did his four younger brothers, whom he helped with their education. All of them became better off than the generation before them. My parents insisted that their children be educated. They wanted us to build on or at least keep the gains they had made. What education has done for my family, it can do for other Africans.

Through education, the young Africans of today can become the teachers, doctors, nurses, scientists, lawyers, engineers, bankers, merchants, entrepreneurs, and civic leaders of tomorrow. Foreign aid in the form of scholarships can do much good, by making professional education accessible to Africans who cannot afford it. Having said this, it is important to point out that education and training is inadequate in and of itself, because professionals move to societies that have political stability and economic opportunity. They need the enabling environment within which to work, and this is where African governments have to step up to the plate.

Unfortunately, this massive project of establishing stability, which should be undertaken by African leaders, is what most foreign aid has been aimed at for decades. Shoring up African governments is the bottomless pit into which billions of aid dollars have gone. But the countries that have assumed the role of sustaining African countries have tried to wield control over many aspects of African life, including, as we have seen, sexual behavior and reproduction rates.

No doubt population control makes some sense from the point of view of the donor: supporting a smaller population costs less than supporting a larger one. And yet, if this way of thinking were extended to an act of personal charity, it would be considered outrageous. If my

neighbors lost everything in a fire, and I included some
condoms in a package of food and blankets I brought
them, they would rightly be offended. So why is it acceptable for wealthy Westerners to send along contraceptives
with their humanitarian aid after a hurricane or another
natural disaster? Trying to stop people in the developing
world from having children should be considered appall-
ing, especially since doing so is not a development strategy. It is an invasion strategy, and that is the reason Africa
must walk away from aid.

The Failure of Aid

If the purpose of foreign aid is to help poor countries to
develop, it has been a failure. In 1974, British economist
Peter Bauer wrote a critical essay for the twenty-fifth anni-
versary of the foreign-aid movement, which he marked
as beginning with United States President Harry Truman
in 1949. Bauer claimed that the movement had failed to
lift countries out of poverty, which was its stated purpose.
He explained that since time immemorial countries have
grown prosperous without the help of foreign aid. To pre-
sume otherwise is offensive, he wrote. "To say that the
peoples of poor countries desperately want material progress but cannot achieve it without alms or gifts from us is
unconscionably patronising. Indeed, a patronising attitude
pervades the whole discussion on aid."[5] Bauer argued that
foreign aid cannot help a country to become richer if the
country lacks the necessary conditions for material progress.
    Although foreign aid cannot cause development, it can
hinder development if it rewards corruption, bad leadership, and dependency, wrote Bauer. Aid often supports

---

[5] Bauer, "Foreign Aid, Forever?", p. 17.

wasteful projects that enrich government leaders and foreign contractors but absorb more local resources than the value of their output. The insistence on the need for external assistance often obscures the necessity for the people of poor countries to develop their own faculties and institutions. Indeed, this insistence on external aid helps to perpetuate the idea that the people are dependent on foreigners for their prosperity. "In this sense aid pauperises those it purports to assist."[6]

Bauer's analysis captures the dynamics of neocolonialism, which are still playing out forty-three years after he made his observations, and his statements have been echoed recently by other credible voices. According to Tom Dichter, who worked with development projects for more than fifty years in more than sixty countries, after seven decades of foreign aid there is little to show for it:

> There are now thousands of ongoing projects that amount to band-aid solutions where the results of "our" interventions disappear almost immediately after the departure of our "expert" teams in their Land Cruisers: new water wells dug in villages where previous donor-built wells have failed; countless capacity-building workshops attended by poor people who are often motivated by the "sitting allowance"—a cash gift; tools given out to farmers who then sell them.[7]

Addressing the anticipated cuts to development aid by the Trump Administration, Dichter continued:

> If aid is cut—even for the wrong reasons—to those nations where the evidence of its ineffectiveness goes back

---

[6] Ibid., p. 19.

[7] Tom Dichter, "I've Worked in Foreign Aid for 50 Years—Trump Is Right to End It, Even If His Reasons Are Wrong", Quartz, April 21, 2017, https://qz.com/959416/time-to-end-foreign-aid-but-for-the-right-reasons/.

decades (almost half of the 48 countries on the UN's Least Developed Countries list have been on it since the list began in 1971, e.g., Haiti, Malawi, Guinea, Benin, Niger, and others), there is a good chance that at least some of these countries will have a real incentive to take charge of their own future.

If Dichter's words fall on deaf ears, the reason might be that the organizations that distribute foreign aid have a vested interest in keeping themselves going:

> At venerable NGOs like Save the Children, World Vision, CARE; at government aid agencies like USAID; at prestigious multilateral organizations like the World Bank; at big foundations like the Bill and Melinda Gates Foundation and the Clinton Foundation; we believe we know what works to better people's lives—we do our homework, we are analytical, thoughtful, and reflective. We are not dumb do-gooders. But what if we are? What if we are neither analytical nor reflective?... And worse, what if we are not even that sincere about doing good? What if we are in the aid business to make sure our own piece of the pie keeps growing?[8]

Perhaps the government leaders who get rich off aid are not the only ones who are corrupt. Even so, Africans cannot take charge of their future until aid, as we know it, is brought to an end, and African leaders unleash the economic potential of their people.

Trade, Not Aid

Pro-market policies are far more important for economic growth than billions of dollars of foreign aid, according to

[8] Ibid.

Andrei Shleifer, professor of economics at Harvard University. The number of people living in absolute poverty has been shrinking rapidly, largely due to the incorporation of developing countries into the world's economy. Since 1970, the number of people living on less than a dollar a day has shrunk from 26 percent to 18 percent of the world's population (which grew enormously), thanks largely to market policies and rapid growth in Asia. The percentage is continuing to fall as more countries join the global economy.[9] Dambisa Moyo, a Zambian economist, identified foreign direct investment, microfinance, and trade as the true routes to development.[10] J. K. Kwakye, an African economist from the Institute of Economic Affairs in Ghana, called for "financial engineering" to mobilize nonaid resources for Africa's development. His proposal includes budget restructuring, development of domestic capital markets, increased mobilization of remittances, issuance of diaspora bonds, securitization of future foreign exchange flows, and reverse capital flight.[11] In these and other analyses, the truth emerges that there is an alternative path to development that is not dependent on foreign aid, and Africans should yearn for this type of development.

Some African leaders are beginning to talk once again about a desire for true independence. A few weeks after his inauguration in 2017, Nana Akufo-Addo, the president of Ghana, expressed a deep desire for economic growth that is not based on "hand-outs" from wealthy donors:

[9] Andrei Shleifer, "Peter Bauer and the Failure of Foreign Aid", *Cato Journal* 29, no. 3 (2009): 389, https://scholar.harvard.edu/files/shleifer/files/bauer_cato _final.pdf.

[10] Dambisa Moyo, *Dead Aid: Why Aid Is Not Working and How There Is a Better Way for Africa* (Vancouver: Douglas and Mcintyre, 2009).

[11] J. K. Kwakye, *Overcoming Africa's Addiction to Foreign Aid: A Look at Some Financial Engineering to Mobilize Other Resources* (Accra, Ghana: Institute of Economic Affairs, 2010), p. 23, http://dspace.africaportal.org/jspui/bitstream /123456789/36121/1/overcoming-africas-addiction-to-foreign-aid.pdf?1.

It was not for nothing that Ghana was the first black African country to break free from colonial rule. We are determined to show that we can emulate the successes of the Asian nations, and, thereby, create a modern, prosperous nation. We believe that a world dominated by a handful of rich nations, with the majority of nations in the south languishing in poverty and misery, is not a prescription for global security. Our generation is not seeking hand-outs from anybody, and neither are we going to be pawns or victims.[12]

The president went on to say that, instead of aid, Africa needs alliances and economic partnerships with the developed world. Here is a man who understands that for Africans not to be the "pawns and victims" of wealthy donors, they need economic growth and independence. He realizes that the path to ideological decolonization begins with economic decolonization.

The Battle over Language

The journey to real freedom and prosperity cannot begin without the people of Africa recognizing the harm being done to their societies by ideological neocolonialism and its link with foreign aid. We need to see beyond the fluffy and seemingly innocuous language of "partnership", "equality", "choice", "diversity", and even "rights", because this language has been redefined to suit a particular ideological worldview. According to this view, killing an unborn baby can be framed as a "safe" abortion; a sexual

[12] Speech by President Alufo-Addo at the New Year greetings with the diplomatic corps, February 16, 2017, website of the Presidency, Republic of Ghana, http://presidency.gov.gh/index.php/2017/02/16/speech-by-president-akufo-addo-at-the-new-year-greetings-with-the-diplomatic-corps/.

relationship between two men can be defined as a "marriage"; and sexual moral standards can be deconstructed in the name of "sexual rights".

An example of the misuse of language can be seen in my 2017 interview with the BBC. The anchor repeatedly referred to contraceptives or access to contraceptives as a woman's "basic human right".[13] I challenged this statement, knowing that basic human rights include life, liberty, and personal security, even according to the Universal Declaration of Human Rights composed by the United Nations.[14] The anchor also insisted that contraception is necessary to lift women out of poverty. When I countered that education was the ticket out of poverty, she argued that contraception was needed along with education. Her unspoken assumptions were that children are the cause of poverty and that childless sex is a human right; thus, contraception (along with abortion) is both a solution to poverty and a human right. She demonstrated perfectly how the use of language in modern Western societies has been constructed to protect these assumptions from being questioned in public discourse. And this use of language is being exported to Africa to undermine the traditional support for abstinence before marriage and fidelity in marriage, which, unlike contraception and abortion, have been proven to promote the health and well-being of individuals and societies.

The power struggle over language in the war on traditional morality was exhibited during the drafting of a

[13] "Nigerian Pro-Life Activist Blasts BBC Anchor for 'Colonial Talk'", Africa News Week, July 16, 2017, https://africanewsweek.com/news/catholic-says-western-countries-who-pay-for-abortion-in-africa-is-a-form-of-ideological-colonisation.

[14] United Nations, Universal Declaration of Human Rights, December 10, 1948, http://www.un.org/en/universal-declaration-human-rights/.

UN resolution about the AIDS crisis. In 2014 a draft of
the resolution was proposed by the delegate from Malawi,
but the Dutch delegate intervened to amend the resolution on behalf of some European countries and the United
States. These Western nations could not accept the mention of "delay of sexual debut" as a way for women to protect themselves from HIV, even though there is a strong
correlation between the age at which unmarried people become sexually active and the incidence of sexually
transmitted diseases. These powerful nations also refused
to tolerate the mention of reducing the number of sexual
partners, even though medical science backs this recommendation. Left in the resolution were condoms, gender
equality, and gender sensitivity. And African countries—
including the primary sponsor Malawi—withdrew their
support and abstained from the vote in protest. Nevertheless, the Dutch version passed by a small margin. "A
disheartened delegate from sub-Saharan Africa, where the
AIDS epidemic has hit hardest, was especially dejected. As
delegates who hijacked the resolution walked by, she said,
'It's all about sex, sex, sex, for them.'"[15]

Indeed, to protect the modern Western delusion that
having all the sex one wants with all the people one wants
is a harmless pastime and an absolute right, language is dis-
carded or redefined at the highest levels of international
bodies. Reality is turned upside down as the protests of
morally conservative individuals, groups, and nations are
ignored and censored. Their representatives in places such
as the United Nation routinely walk away from negotiations discouraged. They often give up before the vote

[15] Rebecca Oas, Ph.D., "Africans Abandon AIDS Resolution after Hijacked
by 'Sexual Progressives'", Center for Family and Human Rights, March
27, 2014, https://c-fam.org/friday_fax/africans-abandon-aids-resolution-after
-hijacked-by-sexual-progressives/.

is counted and, in so doing, cede part of their national sovereignty to their opponents, never mind the harm that is being done to their societies. If Africans are to govern themselves according to their values and to give a bright future to their children, they must learn to fight valiantly against those trying to recolonize them.

The Treasures of African Culture

During a speech for the Organisation of African First Ladies against HIV/AIDS, First Lady of Rwanda Jeannette Kagame urged her counterparts to "look into the depths of the African cultures and create socially responsible initiatives, well-thought-out programmes and campaigns that will encourage prevention and treatment, while fighting (HIV) stigma in communities".[16] I found this statement moving; we do not often hear African leaders publicly acknowledging and even highlighting the relevance of African cultures in tackling modern-day problems. Yet the truth is, if we bother to look within the depths of our cultural heritage, we will find the necessary tools to create "socially responsible" initiatives and "well-thought-out" programs. The widely acknowledged success of Uganda in their fight against AIDS came from such an initiative, built upon cultural values with regard to sexual behavior.

Often I hear Western volunteers and tourists describing Africans as one would describe cute children. With our warmth and our smiles, we seem so happy even in our difficulties, they say. For the most part, Africans are joyful and even jovial, friendly to strangers, welcoming them

---

[16] Athan Tashobya, "Rwanda: First Lady Calls for Renewed Efforts in Fighting HIV/AIDs Prevalence in Africa", *New Times*, February 1, 2017, http://allafrica.com/stories/201702010388.html.

into their homes and offering them a share in the little they have. Africans can indeed seem more content than people from more prosperous countries. The admiration ends, however, with a little pat on the head whenever important decisions are to be made, even over policies that affect the most intimate aspects of our lives. Our cultures and traditions are looked upon as quaint artifacts that have no relevance to the pressing concerns of our times, such as the HIV epidemic.

This kind of condescension was described by Sam L. Ruteikara, the former co-chairman of the Ugandan National AIDS-Prevention Committee:

> In the late 1980s, before international experts arrived to tell us we had it all "wrong," we in Uganda devised a practical campaign to prevent the spread of HIV. We recognized that population-wide AIDS epidemics in Africa were driven by people having sex with more than one regular partner. Therefore, we urged people to be faithful. Our campaign was called ABC (Abstain, or Be Faithful, or use Condoms), but our main message was: Stick to one partner. We promoted condoms only as a last resort....
>
> PEPFAR calls for Western experts to work as equal partners with African leaders on AIDS prevention. But as co-chair of Uganda's National AIDS-Prevention Committee, I have seen this process sabotaged. Repeatedly, our 25-member prevention committee put faithfulness and abstinence into the National Strategic Plan that guides how PEPFAR money for our country will be spent. Repeatedly, foreign advisers erased our recommendations. When the document draft was published, fidelity and abstinence were missing.[17]

[17] Sam L. Ruteikara, "Let My People Go, AIDS Profiteers", *Washington Post*, June 30, 2008, http://www.washingtonpost.com/wp-dyn/content /article/2008/06/29/AR2008062901477.html.

Africans must stand up to patronizing treatment, to Western disregard for the truth of our experience. Our understanding about marriage and family life is backed up by medical science!

The most precious gift that Africans can give to the world right now is our inherent culture of life. Most Africans understand, by faith and tradition, the inestimable value of human life, the beauty of womanhood, the grace of motherhood, the blessing of married life, and the gift of children. All of these have come under great attack in most of the Western world, where abortion on demand is legal, where fertility is considered inconvenient and treated as if it were a disease, where motherhood is devalued and marriage is redefined. Africa can offer the world a refocused view of the dignity of the human person and the goodness of family life, but to do this, we must be confident that we possess something precious. Then more of our leaders will be willing to speak openly and confidently about the treasures of African cultures.

If Western leaders can speak so unabashedly about the right to abortion, as if they are proud of the killing of their unborn, with matching confidence African leaders should speak about the dignity of the unborn child and his right not to be killed. Surely it is more honorable to protect the lives of the innocent and to provide better care for pregnant women so they would not even consider killing their children. This position is more in keeping not only with the cultures and consciences of Africans but with the United Nations' Universal Declaration of Human Rights and its Declaration of the Rights of the Child, which includes the unborn child in a crucial paragraph in its preamble: "*Whereas* the child, by reason of his physical and mental immaturity, needs special safeguards and care, including appropriate legal protection, before as well as after birth."[18] Thus, African leaders should be proud to resist the foreign pressures to legalize abortion.

Threatened Cultural Values Enshrined in Law

Given the social changes—some would even say the social breakdown—occurring in the West, Africans who resist gender ideology and sexual anarchy are truly countercultural. If ever there was a time for them to preserve their cultural norms regarding marriage and family life by encoding them in well-thought-out policies and laws, that time is now. Africans have functional legislative bodies, whose role and prerogative is to make laws that will preserve and protect the dignity of every human life and every family in their countries. They do not need interference from new colonizers; in fact, they must resist it if they are to retain everything they hold dear. Africans have taken for granted that the unborn child has the same right to life as everyone else. But with the rise of the relentless, powerful international abortion industry and its interests being advanced by Western governments and development-aid organizations, there is now a grave necessity for African countries to codify protections for the unborn in their laws. Legislative bodies should pass laws that declare the following:

1. The right to life guaranteed by the national constitution protects each human life and is a person's most fundamental right.

---

[18] Declaration of the Rights of the Child, G.A. res. 1386 (XIV), 14 U.N. GAOR Supp. (No. 16) at 19, UN Doc. A/4354 (1959), https://www.unicef.org/malaysia/1959-Declaration-of-the-Rights-of-the-Child.pdf.

2. Each human life begins with conception or fertiliza-
   tion, at which time a human being has all the legal
   rights accorded with personhood.
3. The legislature, parliament, or assembly has the
   authority to protect all human lives.

Granting the legal rights accorded with personhood to the
unborn child reflects not only the views of large majorities
of African people, but also the objective truth that human
life begins at conception. African nations will do well to
have this reality enshrined in their laws and even etched
into their constitutions where possible.

Uganda added language to protect the unborn child in
its 1995 constitution: "No person has the right to terminate the life of an unborn child except as may be authorised by law."[19] Kenya added the following during its 2010
constitutional review:

1. Every person has the right to life.
2. The life of a person begins at conception.
3. A person shall not be deprived of life intentionally,
   except to the extent authorised by this Constitution
   or other written law.
4. Abortion is not permitted unless, in the opinion of
   a trained health professional, there is need for emergency treatment, or the life or health of the mother
   is in danger, or if permitted by any other written
   law.[20]

---

[19] Uganda's Constitution of 1995 with Amendments through 2005, chap. 4,
sect. 22:2, p. 27, https://www.constituteproject.org/constitution/Uganda_2005
.pdf?lang=en.

[20] Constitution of Kenya (Nairobi: National Council for Law Reporting,
2010), p. 23, http://www.icla.up.ac.za/images/constitutions/kenya_constitution
.pdf.

Both Uganda and Kenya have proven that legal protections of the unborn child can be enshrined in law, and they have set an example that can be followed by other African nations.

The homosexual-rights movement is another front on which African nations must protect themselves from ideological pressure and colonization. This movement has been gaining momentum throughout the world and needs to be stopped in Africa now before it destroys the very thing Africans treasure most—family life. With gender ideology and the sexual confusion it creates, the very definition of human beings as male and female, ordered toward marriage and children, is at stake. If Africans are to preserve marriage and to give a promising future to their children, they must enact socially responsible, well-thought-out, and compassionate marriage and family laws that are based firmly upon the foundations of biological reality and our cultural heritage.

To see how hard this fight will be, one need only look at the United States. In 1996 Congress passed the Defense of Marriage Act, which defined marriage for the purposes of federal law as the union of one man and one woman. It was signed by President Bill Clinton. Less than ten years later, the law was overturned by the Supreme Court. Now is the time for African countries to pass meaningful laws that will formally define marriage as it has been understood for generations, and to fortify themselves against the immense, systematic, and well-funded pressure to legalize same-sex marriage.

If Africa is to protect itself from the social breakdown taking place in the West, which the West is intent on exporting to us, it must stand up for marriage and for children, who are the future of the continent. The corrupting influence of aid from sex-obsessed nations and organizations must be curtailed by building our countries on a firm foundation of good schools that develop not just minds but also character, market economies that free up trade and resources for the benefit of all, and accountable leaders who respect the culture of their people more than the opinion of wealthy donors. We must resist the new ideological colonizers before they rob us of our very selves.

CONCLUSION

I am always inspired when I read stories of how the people of Africa united in the struggle for independence from their Western colonial masters. The decolonization movement was as powerful as it was courageous and was propelled by African leaders who were not afraid to lead their people toward freedom. These African heroes were from different countries, belonged to different ethnic groups, and spoke different languages. They certainly were not perfect, but they were passionate about their cause.

There are many fascinating background stories of this struggle for independence. One of the stories that moves me deeply took place in 1958, when Guinea participated in the referendum on the French constitution—the Constitution of the Fifth Republic. On acceptance of the new constitution, French overseas territories (i.e., colonies) had the options of continuing their existing status as a colony, moving toward full integration into France, or acquiring the status of an autonomous republic in the new French Community (*Communauté française*). If, however, they rejected the new constitution, they would become completely independent. The French president of the time, General Charles de Gaulle, made it clear that any country opting for independence from France would no longer receive French economic aid or retain French technical and administrative officers. Undaunted by this threat, Guinean political leader Ahmed Sékou Touré campaigned vigorously for complete independence from France with the slogan: "We prefer freedom in poverty to opulence in slavery." Thus, in 1958, Guinea voted to sever its ties with France, thereby becoming the first and, in fact, the only French African colony at that time to vote for immediate independence.[1]

In the last fifty years, African nations have tried to hold on to both freedom and donors' opulence. But serving the two masters of self-rule and outsider sponsorship has proven to be impossible, because in spite of what foreign donors tell us foreign aid is not free: it comes with an agenda attached. In a way, Touré was right: the inevitable price of opulence for Africa is slavery, and the most likely consequence of freedom is poverty. Africa's burdens are heavy, and most of them are made heavier by poverty, which makes systemic inadequacies glaring, pandemics severe, and instabilities serious.

My hope is that in this age of infinite possibilities rooted in rapid technological advancement and innovations, Africa will make drastic but necessary changes from within, in order to climb out of poverty. My dream is that one day in the near future the independent nations of Africa will stop depending on their donors' opulence. Like many of the Africans in the 1950s who longed for independence from their colonial masters, I long for independence from our twenty-first-century neocolonial masters so that Africans can rule themselves in a manner that befits their values and aspirations.

---

[1] Mawuna Koutonin, "14 African Countries Forced by France to Pay Colonial Tax for the Benefits of Slavery and Colonization", Silicon Africa, January 28, 2014, http://siliconafrica.com/france-colonial-tax/.

APPENDIX

An African Woman's Open Letter to Melinda Gates

by Obianuju Ekeocha

Growing up in a remote town in Africa, I have always known that a new life is welcomed with much mirth and joy. In fact we have a special "clarion" call (or song) in our village reserved for births and another special one for marriages.

The first day of every baby's life is celebrated by the entire village with dancing (real dancing!) and clapping and singing—a sort of "Gloria in Excelsis Deo".

All I can say with certainty is that we, as a society, *love* and welcome babies.

With all the challenges and difficulties of Africa, people complain and lament their problems openly. I have grown up in this environment and I have heard women (just as much as men) complain about all sorts of things. But I have *never* heard a woman complain about her baby (born or unborn).

The original version of this letter is on the website of the Pontifical Council for the Laity, http://www.laici.va/content/laici/en/sezioni/donna/notizie/an -african-woman-s-open-letter-to-melinda-gates.html.

Even with substandard medical care in most places, women are valiant in pregnancy. And once the baby arrives, they gracefully and heroically rise into the maternal mode.

I trained and worked for almost five years in a medical setting in Africa, yet I never heard of the clinical term "postpartum depression" until I came to live in Europe. I never heard it because I never experienced or witnessed it, even with the relatively high birth rate around me. (I would estimate that I had at least one family member or close friend give birth every single month. So I saw at least twelve babies born in my life every year.)

Amidst all our African afflictions and difficulties, amidst all the socioeconomic and political instabilities, our babies are always a firm symbol of hope, a promise of life, a reason to strive for the legacy of a bright future.

So a few weeks ago I stumbled upon the plan and promise of Melinda Gates to implant the seeds of her "legacy" in sixty-nine of the poorest countries in the world (most of which are in sub-Saharan Africa).

Her pledge is to collect pledges for almost $5 billion in order to ensure that the African woman is less fertile, less encumbered, and, yes, she says, more "liberated". With her incredible wealth she wants to replace the legacy of an African woman (which is her child) with the legacy of "child-free sex".

Many of the sixty-nine targeted countries are Catholic countries with millions of Catholic women of childbearing age. These Catholic women have been rightly taught by the Church that the contraceptive drug or device is inherently divisive.

Unlike what we see in the developed Western world, there is actually very high compliance with Pope Paul VI's *Humanae vitae*. For these African women, in all humility, have heard, understood, and accepted the precious words of the prophetic pope. Funny how people with a much lower literacy level could clearly understand that which the average Vogue- and Cosmo-reading high-class woman has refused to understand. I guess humility makes all the difference.

With most African women faithfully practicing and adhering to a faith (mainly Christian or in some cases Muslim), there is a high regard for sex in society, especially among the women. Sex is sacred and private.

The moment these huge amounts of contraceptive drugs and devices are injected into the roots of our society, they will undoubtedly start to erode and poison the moral sexual ethics that have been woven into our societal DNA by our faith, not unlike the erosion that befell the Western world after the 1930 Lambeth Conference! In one fell swoop and one "clean" slice, the faithful could be severed from their professed faith.

Both the frontline healthcare worker dispensing Melinda's legacy gift and the women fettered and shackled by this gift would be separated from their religious beliefs. They would be put in a precarious position to defy their faith—all for "safe sex".

Even at a glance, anyone could see that the unlimited and easy availability of contraceptives in Africa would surely increase infidelity and sexual promiscuity as sex is presented by this multi-billion-dollar project as a casual pleasure sport that can indeed come with no strings—or babies—attached. Think of the exponential spread of HIV and other STDs as men and women with abundant access to contraceptives take up multiple, concurrent sex partners.

And of course there are bound to be inconsistencies and failures in the use of these drugs and devices, so health complications could result, one of which is unintended abortion. Add also the other health risks such as cancer, blood clots, and so on. Whereas Europe and America have their well-oiled healthcare system, a woman in Africa with a contraception-induced blood clot does not have access to 911 or an ambulance or a paramedic. No, she dies.

And what about disposal of the medical waste? Despite advanced sewage disposal in first-world countries, we hear that aquatic life there is still adversely affected by drugs in the system. In Africa, in both the bigger cities and the smaller rural villages, sewage constitutes a real problem. So as $4.6 billion worth of drugs, IUDs, and condoms get used, they will need safe disposal. Can someone please show us how and where will that be? On our farmlands where we get all our food? In our streams and rivers from whence comes our drinking water?

I see this $4.6 billion buying us misery. I see it buying us unfaithful husbands. I see it buying us streets devoid of the innocent chatter of children. I see it buying us disease and untimely death. I see it buying us a retirement without the tender-loving care of our children.

Please Melinda, listen to the heart-felt cry of an African woman and mercifully channel your funds to pay for what we *really* need:

- Good healthcare systems (especially prenatal, neonatal, and pediatric care)

  Needless to say that postpartum and neonatal deaths are alarmingly high in many sub-Saharan African countries. This is due to the paucity of specialized medical personnel, equipment, and systems. Women are not dying because they are having "too many" babies but because they are not getting even the most basic postpartum care. A childbirth or labor complication can very easily be fatal, for both mother and baby. To alleviate this problem new, well-equipped, well-staffed birthing centers with neonatal units need to be built in easily accessible parts of the poorest communities. And if Melinda Gates really insists on reducing population, she can have highly trained Natural Family Planning (NFP) instructors strategically placed in these women's healthcare facilities. At least then there would be a natural and holistic approach

- Food programs for young children

  These would serve a twofold purpose if they are incorporated into free or highly subsidized nursery school programs. They would nourish and strengthen the growth of children, who are so, so vulnerable to malnutrition, and they would also serve to encourage parents to bring their youngsters, ages three or four, to nursery school. In so many parts of Africa, children miss out on nursery school education because it is expensive and considered a luxury reserved for the rich and the middle class. As a result, children miss the first few crucial years when basic math and reading are easily learned. By the time they are considered ready for school, at age seven or eight, they struggle academically. Many of them never quite catch up and so drop out after six or seven years. This is when a lot of young girls are married off as mid- to late-teenage wives who unfortunately would become the perfect recipient of the Melinda Gates comprehensive contraceptive care!

- Good higher education opportunities

  Not just new school buildings or books, but carefully laid-out educational programs that work—scholarships, internships at higher levels, etc.—are needed. Despite the problems and obstacles to primary and secondary education, a significant number of young girls make it into universities, polytechnics, and colleges. The problem, however, is that most of the schools and resources are substandard and outdated. As such, the quality of higher education is low and cannot compare to that of more privileged countries. Even though the teachers put in their very best and the students work hard, the system is inadequate and will always produce disadvantaged graduates who are not confident enough to stand with their counterparts who have studied in other parts of the world.

- Chastity programs

   Such programs in secondary schools, universities, and churches would create a solid support system to form, inform, and reassure our young girls and women that real love is that which is healthy and holy. Many African girls are no longer sure about moral sexual ethics, thanks to the widespread influence of Western media, movies, and magazines. More support should be given to programs that encourage abstinence before marriage and fidelity in marriage. This approach would go a long way to combating the spread of HIV and other STDs through the continent. And it would certainly lead to happier marriages!

- Support for microbusiness opportunities for women

   The average African women is incredibly happy, hard-working, and resilient. Any support both economic and [educational] through training would most probably be used well and wisely.

- Fortify already established NGOs that are aimed at protecting women from sex-trafficking, prostitution, forced marriage, child labor, domestic violence, sex crimes, etc.

   Many of these NGOs do not have much success because they are not well funded. Though most of them have good intentions, they lack professional input from those such as psychologists, logisticians, and medical personnel needed to tackle various problems.

$4.6 billion dollars can indeed be your legacy to Africa and other poor parts of the world. But let it be a legacy that leads life, love, and laughter into the world in need.

INDEX

Abacha, Sani, 160–61
Abbas, Hakima, 163–64
ABC prevention plan for HIV/
 AIDS, 68–70, 188
Abe, Shinzō, 35
Abedin, Huma, 141–42
abortion: Africans' opposition
 to, 97–99, 101, 118; feminist
 Wangari Maathai on, 83–84;
 illegal abortion in Africa,
 109–10, 113–14, 116–17; and
 maternal mortality rates, 22,
 102–5; Mexico City Policy and
 NGO funding, 145–46, 148–
 49, 169; reasons African women
 seek, 114–16; and second-wave
 Western feminism, 80, 82–83;
 SheDecides campaign to fund
 providers, 146–48. *See also*
 abortion legalization
abortion legalization, 87–95,
 97–118; and African laws
 enshrining legal protections of
 right to life, 190–92; changes in
 abortion law by stealth, 105–13;
 Freetown, Sierra Leone's Safe
 Abortion Bill, 108–13; Imo,
 Nigeria's Abortion Law, 105–7;
 Ipas's 2014 handbook for judges,
 101–2; Kenya's fetal-personhood
 amendment to Constitution,
 140–44; Maputo Protocol and
 the African Union, 86, 87–95;

South Africa's liberal abortion
 law, 109–10; Western donors
 and international organizations
 supporting, 101–2, 106–7,
 108–9, 110–13; where abortion
 is legally permitted for certain
 reasons, 100; where abortion
 is prohibited/allowed only
 to save life of mother, 99;
 where abortion on demand
 is legal, 100–101; WHO's
 2012 publication *Safe Abortion:
 Technical and Policy Guidance
 for Health Systems*, 102; why
 legalization is not the solution,
 116–18
Action Aid International, 87
African Commission on Human
 and People's Rights: *General
 Comment 2 on Article 14* of
 Maputo Protocol, 92–95;
 recommendations on sexual
 and reproductive rights
 education for youth, 94–95;
 and Sierra Leone's 2015 pro-
 abortion bill, 113
African Development Bank, 24
African Feminist Forum in Accra,
 Ghana (2006), 81–82, 84–85
African Union. *See* Maputo
 Protocol
African Women's Development
 Fund (AWDF), 84–85, 86, 87;

African Women's Development
Fund (*continued*)
  *Charter of Feminist Principles for
  African Feminists* at 2006 African
  Feminist Forum, 81–82, 84–85
Agence Française de Développement, 145
aid, foreign (international donors),
  22, 144–48, 157–74, 176–84;
  addiction/dependence on,
  162–65, 174, 176–84; and
  African corruption, 21, 158–62,
  176–77; aid tourism, 24–25;
  condom donations, 71–72,
  152; contraception donations
  and interventions, 166–67,
  170–74; development aid and
  poverty reduction projects,
  180–82; donors' incentives
  to continue, 182; education
  scholarships and professional
  training programs, 178–79;
  failures of, 171–74, 180–82;
  humanitarian aid, 24–25, 178;
  as ideological neocolonialism,
  144–48, 163–65, 181; Mexico
  City Policy and federal funding
  for overseas abortions, 145–46,
  148–49, 169; and philanthropic
  racism, 26–28; population-
  control programs, 27–28,
  40–47, 146–49, 151–53, 165–
  71, 179–80; state-sponsored
  international development
  agencies, 144–49; threats to
  end over homosexuality laws,
  132–36; trade and pro-market
  alternatives, 182–84; and wealth
  of African government officials,
  157–58, 174, 177

Aid to Africa: Redeemer or Coloniser?
  (Abbas), 163–64
Akufo-Addo, Nana, 183–84
Albright, Madeleine, 154
Algeria, 16, 100
American Colonization Society,
  18
American Home Products, 48
Angola, 16, 92, 99
anti-carbon campaign, 149
Association of University Women,
  84
Atlantic Charter, 18–20
Azikiwe, Nnamdi, 19

Baradat, Sergio, 127–28
Bauer, Peter, 177, 180–81
Bayer Healthcare, 48–53; Essure,
  50–53; Yaz and Yasmin birth
  control pills, 48–50
Bellah, Robert, 9
Benin, 16, 100, 173, 182
Berlin Conference (1884–85),
  16
Bibeau, Marie-Claude, 148
Bill and Melinda Gates
  Foundation: contraception
  projects, 25, 40–45, 54–56,
  153–54, 170–71, 198–200;
  population-control agenda
  and Abuja Family Planning
  Conference, 44–45;
  population-control and family-
  planning donations, 85, 146–47,
  168, 170–71; SheDecides
  campaign, 146–48; third-wave
  Western feminist agenda, 85
birth control. *See* contraception
  campaigns; population control
  and family planning programs

BMJ (*British Medical Journal*), 51

Botswana, 16, 91, 100, 104, 109, 161

Bourgi, Robert, 21

breast cancer, 56

British Broadcasting Corporation (BBC), 54–55, 57, 185

British Somaliland, 18

Brockovich, Erin, 52

Buckles, Kasey, 71

Burkina Faso, 16, 48, 54, 100, 173

Burundi, 16, 64, 91, 100

Bush, George W., 145

Cable News Network (CNN), 153–54

Cameroon, 16, 100, 173

Canada, 99, 130, 146–47, 148

Cape Verde, 17, 100, 161

Carter, Jimmy, 154

Catholic Women's Association, 84

Catholicism in Africa, 41

Center for International Policy, 176

Center for Reproductive Rights (CRR), 143–44

Centers for Disease Control and Prevention (U.S.), 139

Central African Republic, 17, 99

Chad, 17, 38, 100, 173

Charter of Feminist Principles for African Feminists (2006), 81–82, 84–85

chastity programs, 202

child marriage, 78–79, 82

Children's Investment Fund Foundation, 54

Chiluba, Frederick, 158–59

Chirac, Jacques, 21

Christian Mother's Guild, 84

Churchill, Winston, 18–19

Clinton, Bill, 145, 154, 192

Clinton, Hillary, 140–42, 154

Cole, Bishop J. Archibald, 112

colonial history of Africa, 14–20; decolonization campaigns led by African leaders, 19–20, 195–96; mid-nineteenth century European scramble for Africa, 15–18; and philanthropic racism, 26–27; post–World War II Atlantic Charter and decolonization, 18–20. *See also* ideological colonialism (Western neocolonialism)

Commonwealth of Nations, 20

Comoros, 17, 100

comprehensive sexuality education (CSE), 60–63, 150–51

Conceptus (manufacturer), 52

condom campaigns: and comprehensive sexuality education (CSE), 62; donations to Africa, 71–72, 152; Ethiopia, 152; failure to prevent death from HIV/AIDS, 66–72; and increased risky sexual behavior, 70–71; Kenya's Global ALL IN campaign ("Condoms for Kids"), 64; Sierra Leone's condom billboards, 151–52; South Africa, 66–67; Uganda, 67–68, 69–70; UNFPA's CONDOMIZE! campaign, 71–72. *See also* population control

Congo-Brazzaville, 17, 99, 160

contraception campaigns, 32–57;
Abuja Family Planning
Conference (2014), 43,
44–47; adverse side effects,
47–57, 199–200; and Africans'
contraceptive use rates/
discontinuation rates, 171–73;
battle over language regarding
human rights, 185; Bayer's
Essure (permanent sterilization
method), 50–53; Bayer's Yaz
and Yasmin birth control pills,
48–50; breast cancer risks, 56;
Cairo Conference (1994), 166–
67; Depo Provero (DMPA),
53–54, 56–57; EAC's bill to
distribute contraceptives to
children and teenagers, 64–65;
failures of, 171–74; Gates
Foundation, 25, 40–45, 53–56,
153–54, 170–71, 198–200; and
HIV-related risks in Africa,
55–56; injectable birth control,
53–57; international donors,
44–57, 166–67, 171–74; and
maternal mortality rates, 43–44;
Norplant, 47–48; Pfizer's
Sayana Press, 54–55; and sexual
promiscuity, 42, 199; and the
Western news media, 153–54.
See also population control
Copenhagen Climate Summit
(2009), 149
corruption and African leaders/
governments, 21, 158–62, 176–
77; Congo-Brazzaville, 160; the
Corruption Perception Index
(CPI), 161–62; Equatorial
Guinea, 160; and illicit capital
flight, 176; and international

donors, 162, 176–77; Malawi,
159, 160; Nigeria, 158, 160–61;
Zambia, 158–59
Corruption Perception Index
(CPI), 161–62
Côte d'Ivoire, 17, 23, 99, 173
Cotonou Agreement, 134–36

Dagen (Norwegian newspaper), 83
Danish International Development
Agency, 106
Danish Ministry of Foreign Affairs,
106
de Gaulle, Charles, 20, 21, 195
Declaration of the Rights of the
Child, 189–90
Democratic Republic of the
Congo, 17, 48, 99
Department for International
Development (UK), 45, 50, 85,
144–45
Depo Provero (DMPA), 53–54,
56–57
Deutsche Gesellschaft für
Internationale Zusammenarbeit
(Germany), 145
development agencies,
international, 144–48. See
also aid, foreign (international
donors)
Dichter, Tom, 181–82
Djibouti, 17, 99
donors, Western. See aid, foreign
(international donors)
drospirenone (synthetic hormone),
49–50
Dusu, Justina, 115
Dutch MDG$_3$, 85
Dutch Ministry of Foreign Affairs,
151

Eads, Brian, 20–21
East African Legislative Assembly's
"Sexual Reproductive Health
and Rights Bill," 64–65
economic colonization. *See* aid,
foreign (international donors)
economies of African nations, 23–
24; mobile phone market, 24;
trade and pro-market alternatives to foreign aid, 182–84
education: comprehensive sexuality
education (CSE), 60–63, 150–
51; foreign aid scholarships and
professional training of young
people, 178–79; the need for
higher education opportunities,
201–2. *See also* sexual-rights
activists and sexuality education
for youth
Egypt, 17, 48, 91, 100, 165
Ehrlich, Paul, 32
Equality Now, 86, 89–90
Equatorial Guinea, 17, 100, 160
Eritrea, 17, 100
Essure (permanent sterilization
method), 50–53
Ethiopia, 17, 33–34, 100, 149, 152,
173
Ethiopian Women Lawyers
Association, 89
European Commission's
Directorate-General for
International Cooperation and
Development, 145
European Union: Cotonou Agree-
ment, 134–36; normalization
of homosexuality, 121, 127,
134–36
expressive individualism, 9–11
Ezekwesili, Oby, 161

Family Care International, 86
family planning, 27–29; as term,
45–46; USAID's "family
planning priority countries,"
28. *See also* contraception
campaigns; population control
Family Planning 2020, 46
Federation of Business and
Professional Women, 84
Federation of Muslim Women's
Association, 84
Federation of Women Lawyers–
Kenya, 144
female genital mutilation (FGM),
78–79, 82, 123
feminism, radical Western, 79–84;
and abortion legalization,
80; and African women, 77–95;
and African women's beauty
and resilience, 77–78; AWDF,
84–85, 87; *Charter of Feminist
Principles for African Feminists*
at 2006 African Feminist
Forum in Accra, 81–82, 84–85;
emerging African women's
organizations, 84–87; failure to
recognize women's traditional
roles, 82–83; FEMNET,
85–86, 87, 89, 111; first-wave,
80; Maathai and, 83–84;
Maputo Protocol and women's
rights, 86, 87–95; model of
womanhood being imposed
on Africa, 78; the need for
authentic feminism, 78–79,
89; second-wave, 80, 82–83;
SOAWR, 86–87, 91; support
for commercial sex work and
pornography, 81; third-wave,
80–87; traditional African

feminism, radical Western
(*continued*)
  women's organizations, 84;
  and violence against women,
  115–16
FEMNET (African Women's
  Development and
  Communication Network),
  85–86, 87, 89, 111
Ferguson, Sian, 109–10
fertility rates, 31–37, 147; African
  women's desired, 37–40;
  alarmism about population
  explosion, 31–37; of Western
  donor-countries, 147. *See also*
  population control
Filipovic, Jill, 38–39
Food and Drug Administration
  (FDA), U.S., 49–50, 51–52,
  56
food programs for young children,
  201
Ford Foundation, 85, 87, 106, 168
France: foreign policy of Françafrique, 20–21; investigation of
  Francophone African leaders
  for embezzlement, 159–60;
  population-control funding,
  168; secretary of international
  development, 59–60; support
  of LGBT agenda, 130; Touré's
  campaign for Guinea's independence from, 19–20, 195–96
Fred Hutchinson Cancer Research
  Center (Seattle), 56
Fredskorpset, 86
Free and Equal Campaign of the
  UNPA, 127–29

Gabon, 17, 99
Gambia, The, 17, 91, 99

Gates, Melinda: contraception
  projects through Gates
  Foundation, 25, 40–45, 153–54,
  170–71, 198–200; Ekeocha's
  Open Letter to, 41–43,
  197–203
Gates Foundation. *See* Bill and
  Melinda Gates Foundation
Gelander, Gunilla Pettersson, 177
George, Robert P., 9–11
George VI, King, 14–15
Ghana, 17, 48, 52, 100;
  alternative paths to economic
  development, 183–84;
  contraception prevalence rate,
  44, 173; desired number of
  children, 37; disapproval of
  abortion, 98; disapproval
  of homosexual lifestyles, 123;
  first African Feminist Forum
  in Accra (2006), 81–82; GDP,
  23; legislators' pay, 158
Global Affairs Canada, 144–45
Global Financial Integrity, 161–62
Global Fund, 64, 70, 152
Global Fund for Women, 85, 87,
  106
Gore, Al, 154
Gosnell, Kermit, 154
Government Accountability Office
  (U.S.), 142
Green, Edward, 70–71
*Guidelines for Reducing Morbidity and
  Mortality from Unsafe Abortion*
  (Kenya), 143–44
Guinea, 17, 100, 173, 182; Touré's
  campaign for independence
  from France, 19–20, 195–96
Guinea-Bissau, 17, 99
Guttmacher Institute, 22, 109,
  150–51

Halivura, Betty, 114
Hanlon, Joseph, 162
Harvard AIDS Prevention Project, 70
Hassan, Mariama, 39
healthcare systems for women, 200–201
Healthy, Happy and Hot: A Young Person's Guide to Their Rights, Sexuality and Living with HIV (IPPF, 2010), 73–75
Hewlett Foundation, 168
History of Africa (Shillington), 16
HIV/AIDS epidemic in Africa, 65–75, 124, 185–88; ABC prevention plan and abstinence, 68–70, 188; drafting language of 2014 UN AIDS resolution, 185–87; failure of condom campaigns, 66–72; Kenya's Global ALL IN campaign ("Condoms for Kids"), 64; looking to African culture to tackle problem of, 187–88; mother-to-child transmission, 66; and risks of injectable birth control, 55–56; South Africa, 66–67; strategy of decriminalizing prostitution, 72–73; strategy of destigmatizing HIV, 73–75; transmission and death toll, 65–66; Uganda, 67–70, 187–88; UNFPA's CONDOMIZE! campaign, 71–72; women's infection rates, 66
Hivos, 86, 87
Hohn, Chris, 146
homophobia, 125–26
homosexuality, normalization of, 47, 119–36; African parents' love for children who struggle with same-sex attraction, 124–25, 127; Africans labeled as homophobic, 122, 125–26; Africans' disapproval of homosexual lifestyles, 122–24; Africa's responses to Western interference, 131–36; commemorative postage stamps and propaganda platforms, 127–29; European Union, 121, 127, 134–36; human rights agenda/sexual-rights recommendations of the UN-UPR, 129–31; and mob violence (vigilantism), 125–26; Obama and, 122–24, 132–34; protecting African values by enactment of marriage definitions and laws, 192–93; U.S. Supreme Court's ruling on same-sex marriage, 121; Western countries' threats to suspend aid over anti-homosexuality laws, 132–36. *See also* sexual-rights activists and sexuality education for youth
Houphouët-Boigny, Félix, 19
Human Rights and African Abortion Laws: A Handbook for Judges (Ipas Africa Alliance), 101–2
Humanae vitae (Paul VI), 41, 198–99
humanitarian-aid tourism, 24–25
Hungerman, Daniel, 71

ideological colonialism (Western neocolonialism), 9–11, 25–29, 137–55, 175–93, 195–96; and African posture of obedience and deference, 21–22; the battle

ideological colonialism (*continued*)
  over language, 184–87; and
  expressive individualism, 9–11;
  foreign aid as, 163–65, 181;
  France's policy of Françafrique,
  20–21; paternalism and
  unsolicited interventionism,
  138–44; reversing, 175–93;
  Western condescension
  and patronizing treatment,
  187–89; Western hypocrisy,
  155; the Western news media,
  153–55; Western organizations'
  infiltration of African
  institutions, 150–55. *See also* aid,
  foreign (international donors)
Igbo language of Nigeria, 97–98
Imo Abortion Law (Nigeria), 105–7
Institute for Pregnancy Loss
  (Jacksonville, Florida), 116
International AIDS Conference
  (2014) (Melbourne, Australia),
  72–73
International Conference on
  Population and Development
  (ICPD) in Cairo (1994),
  165–67, 168, 169–70
International Development Law
  Organization (IDLO), 142–43
International Lesbian, Gay,
  Bisexual, Transgender, and
  Intersex Association, 130
International Monetary Fund
  (IMF), 23
International Planned Parenthood
  Federation (IPPF), 10, 45,
  50, 86; *Healthy, Happy
  and Hot* (2010) and HIV
  destigmatization, 73–75; and
  Mexico City Policy, 145

International Women's Health
  Coalition, 86
Inter-Religious Council of Sierra
  Leone (IRCSL), 112
Ipas Africa Alliance: abortion rights
  agenda, 86, 93–94, 101–2, 110–
  11; and Abuja Family Planning
  Conference, 45; handbook for
  judges, 101–2; and Maputo
  Protocol, 93–94
Ipsos, 98, 153
Italian Somaliland, 18
It's All One curriculum (Popula-
  tion Council), 61–62

Japan, 35–36, 168

Kabia, Isatu, 108
Kagame, Jeannette, 187
Kenya, 17, 48, 52, 54, 56, 91,
  100, 114, 115, 149, 173; births
  to unmarried women, 140;
  Constitutional protections of
  right to life, 140–44, 191–92;
  disapproval of homosexual
  lifestyles, 123; domestic
  violence, 115; Global ALL
  IN campaign ("Condoms
  for Kids"), 64; Guttmacher
  Institute's study of sexuality
  education in, 150–51;
  disapproval of abortion, 98;
  legislators' pay, 158; lynching
  statistics, 126; Maathai on
  abortion in, 83
Kenyan Committee of Experts,
  142
Kenyatta, Jomo, 19
Kerry, John, 154
Kipling, Rudyard, 26–27

Kizito, Monica, 65
Koroma, Ernest, 112–13
Kreditanstalt für Wiederaufbau
    (German development bank),
    50
Kwakye, J. K., 183

Lagos, Nigeria, 36–37
Lancet, 55–56
Leading Safe Choices, 110
lesbian, gay, bisexual, and trans-
    gender (LGBT) identity. *See*
    homosexuality, normalization
    of
Lesotho, 17, 99
Liberia, 16, 17, 91, 100, 173
Libya, 17, 91, 99
Likimani, Naisola, 93–94
Luka, Stephen, 115
lynching, 126

Maathai, Wangari, 83–84
MacArthur Foundation, 45, 106
Madagascar, 17, 48, 99
Maiga, Soyata, 92–93
Maila, Joe, 110
Malawi, 17, 48, 99; anti-corruption
    campaign and "Cashgate"
    (2013), 160; corruption by
    President Muluzi, 159; foreign
    aid and national budget, 163;
    lynching statistics, 126; UN
    delegation and drafting of 2014
    UN AIDS resolution, 186
Maldives, 43–44
Mali, 17, 100, 173
Mama Cash, 85, 87, 106
Mandela, Nelson, 109
Maputo Protocol, 86, 87–95;
    African Commission's *General*

Comment 2 on Article 14,
    92–95; article 14 and abortion
    rights, 88, 89–95; countries
    registering reservations, 91;
    impact on abortion law in
    member countries, 91–94;
    and Ipas Africa Alliance,
    93–94; recommendations
    aimed at healthcare workers
    and midwives, 95; SOAWR
    campaigns for ratification,
    86, 91; twenty-five articles
    addressing women's rights,
    88–89
Marie Stopes International (MSI),
    25, 45, 50, 145
Mark, David, 132
marriage: Africans' commitment
    to family life and, 122–24;
    child marriage, 78–79, 82, 89;
    enactment of definitions and
    laws to protect, 192–93; Igbo
    tradition, 119–20; polygamous,
    124; U.S. Defense of Marriage
    Act (1996), 192; U.S. Supreme
    Court's 2015 ruling on same-
    sex, 121
Match International Women's
    Fund, Canada, 85
maternal mortality rates: and
    abortion, 22, 102–5; actual
    causes of maternal deaths,
    103–4; and birth rates, 43–44;
    and misplaced priorities of
    abortion advocates, 102–5;
    postpartum bleeding, 104;
    South Africa, 109
Mauritania, 17, 99
Mauritius, 17, 100, 161
May, John, 32

2

14 TARGET AFRICA

media, Western: and ideological
colonialism, 153–55;
population-control and
contraception campaigns, and
reactions to African views
on homosexuality, 125, 133,
153–54; view of Africans as
people in need, 24–25
Mexico City Policy, 145–46,
148–49, 169
microbusiness opportunities for
women, 202
mob violence (vigilantism), 125–26
Mohammed, Lai, 161
Mohammed, Zakari, 132
Morocco, 17, 100
Moss, Todd, 177
Moyo, Dambisa, 183
Mozambique, 17, 91, 100, 111
Mugahi, Paul, 114
Muluzi, Bakili, 159

Namibia, 17, 91, 100, 161
National Institutes of Health, 56,
134
Natural Family Planning (NFP),
201
natural resources, Africa's, 23
neocolonialism. *See* ideological
colonialism (Western
neocolonialism)
Network of African Rural
Women's Association, 84
New York Times, 55–56
news media. *See* media, Western
Niger, 32, 37–39, 54, 56, 100, 173
Nigeria, 17, 99; author's
experience of growing up in
postcolonial, 13–15; births
to unmarried women, 140;

contraception and family
planning programs, 43;
disapproval of abortion, 98;
disapproval of homosexual
lifestyles, 123; government
corruption cases, 158, 160–61;
homosexuality laws and
Western threats to suspend aid,
132–35; Igbo names, 97–98;
Imo Abortion Law, 105–7;
international Family Planning
Conference in Abuja (2014),
43, 44–47; legislators' wealth,
157–58; mass urban migration
and urbanization, 36–37; mob
violence, 126; national anthem,
13–14
Nigeria Family Planning Blueprint,
43
Nigeria Family Planning
Conference in Abuja (2014),
43, 44–47
Nigeria's Economic and Financial
Crimes Commission, 158
Nkrumah, Kwame, 19
nongovernmental organizations
(NGOs), 9–10; donors to
population-control and family
planning programs, 167–71;
fortifying established women's
organizations, 203; the Ipas
Africa Alliance and abortion
legalization, 93–94; Mexico
City Policy and funding for
abortions, 145–46, 148–49, 169
Norplant, 47–48
Norwegian Agency for
Development Cooperation, 85,
106, 145
Nyerere, Julius, 19

Obama, Barack: efforts to influence normalization of homosexuality in Africa, 122–24, 132–34; Ekeocha's open letter to, 123–24; Mexico City Policy, 145; Senegal visit (2013), 122–24; threat to cut off aid to Nigeria, 132–33; and Uganda's anti-sodomy law, 133–34

Okorocha, Rochas, 105, 107

Omole, Tosin, 132–33

Open Society Foundations, 85, 87

Opondo, Ofwono, 136

Organisation of African First Ladies against HIV/AIDS, 187

Oxfam GB, 87, 91

Oxfam Novib, 85, 87

Packard Foundation, 168

Pathfinder, 45

Paul VI, Pope, 41, 198–99

Pearce, Fred, 34

Pentecostal Fellowship of Sierra Leone, 112

Pew Research Center surveys on views on morality in Africa, 63, 98–99, 101, 122–23

Pfizer Inc., 54–55, 56–57

Planned Parenthood. See International Planned Parenthood Federation (IPPF); Planned Parenthood Federation of America

Planned Parenthood Federation of America, 140–44, 154

political leaders, African: corruption and, 158–62, 176–77; wealth of, 157–58, 174, 177; women as, 23

polygamous marriage, 124

PopOffsets (website), 149

The Population Bomb (Ehrlich), 32

population control and family planning programs, 27–28, 31–57; Abuja Family Planning Conference (2014), 43, 44–47; and African women's desired fertility rate, 37–40; and African women's sexual ethics, 41–42; and Africa's uncontrolled urbanization, 36–37; alarmism about population explosion, 31–37; Cairo Conference on Population and Development (1994), 165–67, 168, 169–70; contraceptive donation programs, 44–57, 166–67, 170–71; demographic decline in developed world, 34–36; foreign aid and donors, 27–28, 40–47, 147–48, 151–53, 165–71, 179–80; increases in funding, 169–70; and maternal mortality rates, 43–44, 103–4; philanthropic racism, 26–28; rhetoric of the "unmet need" for family planning, 38–40; SheDecides campaign, 146–48; the term "family planning," 45–46; USAID's "family planning priority countries," 28; and the Western media (CNN), 153–55. See also contraception campaigns

Population Council's It's All One curriculum, 61–62

Population Matters (anti-carbon campaign), 149

Population Reference Bureau, 32

Population Services International, 50

postpartum depression, 40, 198

Prager, Dennis, 117

President's Emergency Plan for AIDS Relief (PEPFAR), 188

prostitution ("sex work"), 115; decriminalization of, 72–73; and third-wave feminism, 80–81

racism, philanthropic, 26–28

Reagan, Ronald, 145

Rockefeller Foundation, 168

Roosevelt, Franklin D., 18–19

Royal College of Obstetricians & Gynecologists, 110

Rubiner, Laurie, 140–42

Ruteikara, Sam L., 69–70, 188

Rwanda, 18, 48, 64, 91, 100, 161, 173; female parliamentarians, 23; First Lady Kagame's speech on fight against HIV/AIDS, 187

Safe Abortion: Technical and Policy Guidance for Health Systems (WHO, 2012), 102

Sall, Mackay, 122

São Tomé and Príncipe, 18, 99

Saraki, Bukalo, 126

Sarki, Usman, 128–29

Sayana Press (injectable contraceptive), 54–55

secular progressivism, 10–11

Senegal, 18, 54, 91, 99, 122, 173

sexually transmitted diseases, 62, 139, 151. *See also* HIV/AIDS epidemic in Africa

sexual-rights activists and sexuality education for youth, 59–75; the African Commission's education recommendations, 94–95; and Africans' conservative moral views, 63; comprehensive sexuality education (CSE), 60–63, 150–51; condom campaigns, 66–72; EAC's contraception-distribution bill, 64–65; and HIV/AIDS epidemic, 65–75; international efforts to influence the "political will" on Africa, 63–65; IPPF's 2010 publication to destigmatize life with HIV, 73–75; Kenya's Global ALL IN campaign ("Condoms for Kids"), 64; Population Council's *It's All One* curriculum, 61–62; teaching condom use, 62; teaching masturbation, 61–62. *See also* HIV/AIDS epidemic in Africa; homosexuality, normalization of

Seychelles, 18, 100

Shamim, Ismail, 117

SheDecides campaign, 146–48

Shillington, Kevin, 16

Shleifer, Andrei, 183

Sidze, Estelle, 150–51

Sierra Leone, 18, 99; condom billboards as population-control projects, 151–52; Ebola crisis, 108; Freetown's Safe Abortion Bill (2015), 108–13

Sigrid Rausing Trust, 87

slums, 37

SOAWR (Solidarity for African Women's Rights), 86–87, 91

Somalia, 99

South Africa, 18, 100; condom program, 66–67; HIV incidence

rates, 66–67; illegal abortions/
    registered abortions, 109–10;
    liberal abortion law (Choice
    on Termination of Pregnancy
    Act), 109–10; lynching
    incidents, 126; maternal
    mortality rate, 109; views of
    abortion, 101
South Sudan, 99, 117
Soviet Union, 80
Sudan, 18, 64, 91, 100
Swaziland, 18, 100
Sweden, Embassy of, 86, 87
Swedish Association for Sexuality
    Education, 86
Swedish International Develop-
    ment Cooperation Agency
    (Sida), 106, 145, 148–49, 151

Tanzania, 18, 48, 64, 91, 99, 149,
    173; maternal mortality rate,
    43–44
Telegraph, 33
Togo, 18, 100, 173
Touré, Ahmed Sékou, 19–20,
    195–96
Transparency International, 161
Trudeau, Justin, 147
Truman, Harry, 180
Trump, Donald: cuts to
    development aid, 181–82;
    Mexico City Policy, 145, 146,
    169
Tunisia, 18, 91, 100; disapproval
    of homosexual lifestyles, 123;
    views of abortion, 98, 101

Uganda, 18, 99; condom
    campaigns, 67–68, 69–70;
    constitutional protections of the

unborn child (1995), 191–92;
    disapproval of homosexual
    lifestyles, 123; HIV/AIDS
    epidemic and prevention
    campaigns, 67–70, 187–88;
    homosexuality laws and
    Western threats to suspend
    aid, 133–35, 136; lynching
    statistics, 126; tax collection and
    addiction to foreign aid, 164
Ugandan National AIDS-
    Prevention Committee, 69–70,
    188
UN Commission on Population
    and Development (2017),
    59–60
UN Convention on the
    Elimination of All Forms of
    Discrimination against Women
    (2014), 108
United Kingdom: population
    density, 33–34; population-
    control programs and
    family planning assistance in
    developing world, 27–28, 170
United Nations: Charter, 128;
    Declaration of the Rights of
    the Child, 188–89; pro-LGBT
    commemorative stamps,
    127–29; Universal Declaration
    of Human Rights, 185, 189
United Nations Children's Fund
    (UNICEF), 62, 64
United Nations Department of
    Economic and Social Affairs
    (UN DESA), 31–33
United Nations Education,
    Scientific, and Cultural
    Organization (UNESCO), 62,
    150

United Nations Joint Program
for HIV/AIDS (UNAIDS):
condom campaigns, 70;
international guidelines for
comprehensive sexuality
education (CSE), 62; Kenya's
Global ALL IN campaign, 64
United Nations Population
Fund (UNFPA), 33, 50, 167;
and Abuja Family Planning
Conference, 45; condom
campaigns, 70, 71–72, 152;
international guidelines for
comprehensive sexuality
education (CSE), 62; Kenya's
Global ALL IN campaign, 64;
recommendations on use of
DMPA (Depo Provera), 53–54
United Nations Postal
Administration (UNPA),
127–29
United Nations Women, 85
United States: births to unmarried
women, 139–40; Defense of
Marriage Act (1996), 192;
and Kenya's fetal-personhood
amendment, 140–44;
Mexico City Policy, 145–46,
148–49, 169; normalization
of homosexuality, 121,
122–24, 132–34; population-
control programs and
family planning assistance in
developing world, 168–69,
170; sexual permissiveness and
STDs, 139; Supreme Court
ruling establishing right to
homosexual marriage, 121;
unsolicited intervention in
Africa, 140–44

United States Agency for International Development
(USAID), 144; contraception
donations, 50; family planning
priority countries, 28;
population-control agenda
and Abuja Family Planning
Conference, 45; report on
desired number of children
in African countries, 37–38;
survey on contraception
discontinuation, 171–72
Universal Declaration of Human
Rights, 185, 189
UN-UPR (Universal Periodic
Review), 129–31
Upadhyay, Jagdish, 33
urbanization, 36–37
Urgent Action Fund–Africa, 85

van de Walle, Nicholas, 177
Vatican's Pontifical Council for the
Laity, 41
vesicovaginal fistula, 78
violence: mob violence (vigilantism) against homosexuals,
125–26; against women,
115–16

Wandia, Mary, 89–90
"We Are the World" (1985 song),
25–26
wealth of African government
officials, 157–58, 174, 177. See
also corruption and African
leaders/governments
"White Man's Burden, The"
(Kipling), 26–27
WomanCare Global, 52–53
Women in Aviation, 84

Women's Foundation of
    Minnesota, 85
Women's Funding Network,
    U.S.A., 85
Women's Global Network
    for Reproductive Rights
    (WGNRR), 106–7
World Health Organization
    (WHO): analysis of maternal
    mortality, 103–4; guidelines
    for comprehensive sexuality
    education, 62; Kenya's Global
    ALL IN campaign, 64; *Safe*

*Abortion: Technical and Policy
    Guidance for Health Systems*
    (2012), 102
World War II, 18–20

Yaz and Yasmin (birth control
    pills), 48–50

Zambia, 18, 48, 91, 100, 158–59,
    183
Zimbabwe, 18, 44, 48, 100, 173
Zucker, Jeff, 153